Learning PHP Data Objects

A Beginner's Guide to PHP Data Objects, Database
Connection Abstraction Library for PHP 5

Dennis Popel

BIRMINGHAM - MUMBAI

Learning PHP Data Objects

First published: September 2007

Production Reference: 2310807

Published by Packt Publishing Ltd.
32 Lincoln Road
Olton
Birmingham, B27 6PA, UK.

ISBN 978-1-847192-66-0

www.packtpub.com

Cover Image by Derek Heasley (the_matrix@eircom.net)

Credits

Author

Dennis Popel

Reviewers

Dinangkur Kundu

Tahmid Munaz

Acquisition Editors

Nanda Padmanabhan

Viraj Joshi

Development Editor

Rashmi Phadnis

Technical Editor

Swapna.V.Verlekar

Project Manager

Abhijeet Deobhakta

Editorial Manager

Dipali Chittar

Project Coordinator

Zenab Ismail Kapasi

Indexer

Bhushan Pangaonkar

Proofreaders

Martin Brooks

Chris Smith

Production Coordinators

Shantanu Zagade

Manjiri Nadkarni

Cover Designer

Shantanu Zagade

About the Author

Dennis Popel is an experienced PHP/PHP 5 developer currently working for an Australian web development company, Motive Media (www.motivemedia.com.au). Serving Sun Microsystems Australia, Luna Park Sydney, Alsco Holdings, and Pine Solutions, among others, Dennis leads company development of proprietary, web-based, software solutions. In his spare time, he runs the www.onphp5.com blog and works on an online RSS aggregator newzmix.com.

Dennis Popel has been developing with PHP for more than 5 years and is experienced in such fields as object-oriented design and MVC. Previously he has worked at Rapid Intelligence, another Australian-based web company, publisher of such popular titles as NationMaster.com, FactBites.com, and Qwika.com. In the past, Dennis was developing proprietary Java applications.

This book is devoted to all the people who introduced and guided me in this wonderful world of information technology.

About the Reviewers

Dinangkur Kundu completed his bachelor's degree in Information Technology from Central Queensland University, Australia. He has been working as a software engineer and network admin—designing, developing, and configuring. He has worked with a variety of 2nd, 3rd, and 4th generation languages. He has worked with flat files, indexed files, hierarchical databases, network databases, and relational databases, several Sun and HP servers to configure small and medium range office networks providing Internet service, Mail service, file share service, network-based printing service, backup service, and implementing several network-based applications. Currently, he works as Chief Technical Officer at Quantumcloud, developing and customizing LAMP- and WAMP-based web services. He enjoys producing high-quality software, web-based solutions, and designing secure network.

I would like to thank my family for supporting and inspiring my ongoing passion for software development and the resultant challenges of life near the bleeding edge. I would also like to thank Mr. Jamil and Mr. Hasin, my close professional mentors and who to this day remain close friends. You can contact me at dkundu@gmail.com.

Tahmid Munaz is currently working in Relisource Technologies (www.relisource.com) as an SQA Engineer. He is also a volunteer in an association called SQABD (SQA Bangladesh—www.sqabd.com) as a Community Relations Manager. He has experience in conducting QA and Testing training and mentoring freshers for Testing and QA Career paths and Consulting.

He loves to keep in touch with other Technical Communities like—JPGroup, Dot_net_community, PHPExpert, and PHPResource. He is addicted to reading blogs and writing when he gets time. You can visit Tahmid's blog at http://tahmidmunaz.blogspot.com

I would like to thank Hasin, the author of "Wordpress Complete", who always inspired me. Thanks to my friend Mizan, the author of "MediaWiki Administrators' Tutorial Guide", who helped me in my reviewing as it was first time for me. Thanks to the Packt team for giving me the support for this startup, especially to Viraj, Rashmi, and Abhijeet. I really enjoyed reviewing and hope to do better in future. I had heard about the author of this book but had no chance to work together. It was a chance for me to work with him and feel proud to help him make a nice book. I would like to thank my Program Managers who have always helped me to do and learn in better ways: Sahadatul Hakim (Enosis Solutions).

Table of Contents

Preface

This book will introduce you to one of the most important extensions to PHP that are available, starting with PHP version 5.0 — the PHP Data Objects, commonly known as PDO.

PHP grew in to a very popular web programming language due to its simplicity and ease of use. One of the key factors of this growing success is the built-in possibility to access many popular relational database management systems (RDBMS), such as MySQL, PostgreSQL, and SQLite, to name just a few. Today, most of the existing and newly created web applications interconnect with these databases to produce dynamic, data-driven websites.

While most PHP-enabled web servers are still running PHP versions prior to 5.0, the enhancements and performance improvements introduced with this new version will lead to wide acceptance of PHP 5 at all levels during coming years. This imposes the need to start familiarizing ourselves with all the advanced features available in this version today.

What This Book Covers

Chapter 1 gives an overview of PDO along with a few features likes single interface for creating a connection, connection strings, uniform statement methods, and use of exceptions and a singe system of error codes.

Chapter 2 helps to get you started with PDO, by creating a sample database and then by creating a connection object. It also introduces PDOStatement classes.

Chapter 3 deals with various error-handling processes and their uses.

Chapter 4 introduces prepared statements. It deals with using prepared statements without binding values, binding a variable, and binding a parameter to a prepared statement. We also take a look at how to work with BLOBs using streams so that we do not risk query failures.

Chapter 5 helps us determine the number of rows in the returned result set. Also, we come across a new concept—scrollable cursors, which allow us to fetch subsets of rows from a result set.

Chapter 6 talks about advanced uses of PDO and includes setting connection parameters, transactions, and methods of PDO and the PDOStatement class.

Chapter 7 gives an example, where creation of the method part of an MVC application is discussed.

Appendix A explains the object-oriented features like inheritance, encapsulation, polymorphism, and exception handling.

Who This Book is For

This book is targeted at PHP programmers, who are considering migrating to PHP 5 and using the new database connection abstraction library, PHP Data Objects. While PDO is fully object oriented, the familiarity with this programming paradigm is required. Novice users who are not familiar with PHP 5's object-oriented features may consider reading Appendix A first so that they can follow the code examples in this book.

We assume that the reader is familiar with SQL, at the level of creating tables and making simple SELECT queries as well as updates. Our examples are based on MySQL and SQLite databases as these are the most used options and the only ones available at most cheap hosting providers.

At the end of this book we will present a more advanced example which may be of interest to expert programmers with deeper knowledge of SQL and programming concepts.

Conventions

In this book, you will find a number of styles of text that distinguish between different kinds of information. Here are some examples of these styles, and an explanation of their meaning.

There are three styles for code. Code words in text are shown as follows: "PostgreSQL users might have already used pg_prepare() and pg_execute() pair."

A block of code will be set as follows:

```
// Assume we also want to filter by make
$sql = 'SELECT * FROM cars WHERE make=?';
$stmt = $conn->prepare($sql);
$stmt->execute(array($_REQUEST['make']));
```

When we wish to draw your attention to a particular part of a code block, the relevant lines or items will be made bold:

```
// Assume we also want to filter by make
$sql = 'SELECT * FROM cars WHERE make=?';
$stmt = $conn->prepare($sql);
$stmt->execute(array($_REQUEST['make']));
```

New terms and **important words** are introduced in a bold-type font. Words that you see on the screen, in menus or dialog boxes for example, appear in our text like this: "You can simply click on the **Authors** link located on the books listing page in your browser ".

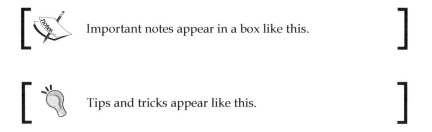

Important notes appear in a box like this.

Tips and tricks appear like this.

Reader Feedback

Feedback from our readers is always welcome. Let us know what you think about this book, what you liked or may have disliked. Reader feedback is important for us to develop titles that you really get the most out of.

To send us general feedback, simply drop an email to feedback@packtpub.com, making sure to mention the book title in the subject of your message.

If there is a book that you need and would like to see us publish, please send us a note in the **SUGGEST A TITLE** form on www.packtpub.com or email suggest@packtpub.com.

If there is a topic that you have expertise in and you are interested in either writing or contributing to a book, see our author guide on www.packtpub.com/authors.

Customer Support

Now that you are the proud owner of a Packt book, we have a number of things to help you to get the most from your purchase.

Downloading the Example Code for the Book

Visit http://www.packtpub.com/support, and select this book from the list of titles to download any example code or extra resources for this book. The files available for download will then be displayed.

The downloadable files contain instructions on how to use them.

Errata

Although we have taken every care to ensure the accuracy of our contents, mistakes do happen. If you find a mistake in one of our books—maybe a mistake in text or code—we would be grateful if you would report this to us. By doing this you can save other readers from frustration, and help to improve subsequent versions of this book. If you find any errata, report them by visiting http://www.packtpub.com/support, selecting your book, clicking on the **Submit Errata** link, and entering the details of your errata. Once your errata are verified, your submission will be accepted and the errata added to the list of existing errata. The existing errata can be viewed by selecting your title from http://www.packtpub.com/support.

Questions

You can contact us at questions@packtpub.com if you are having a problem with some aspect of the book, and we will do our best to address it.

1
Introduction

PHP Data Objects, (PDO) is a PHP5 extension that defines a lightweight DBMS connection abstraction library (sometimes called data access abstraction library). The need for a tool like PDO was dictated by the great number of database systems supported by PHP. Each of these database systems required a separate extension that defined its own API for performing the same tasks, starting from establishing a connection to advanced features such as preparing statements and error handling.

The fact that these APIs were not unified made transition between underlying databases painful, often resulting in the rewriting of many lines of code, which in turn, led to new programming errors that required time to track, debug and correct. On the other hand, the absence of a unified library, like JDBC for Java, was putting PHP behind the big players in the programming languages world. Now that such library exists, PHP is regaining its position and is a platform of choice for millions of programmers.

It should be noted, however, that there exist several libraries written in PHP, that serve the same purpose as PDO. The most popular are the ADOdb library and the PEAR DB package. The key difference between them and PDO is speed. PDO is a PHP extension written in a compiled language (C/C++), while the PHP libraries are written in an interpreted language. Also, once PDO is enabled, it does not require you to include source files in your scripts and redistribute them with your application. This makes installing your applications easier, as the end user does not need to take care of third-party software.

 Here, we are neither comparing these libraries with PDO nor advocating the use of PDO over such libraries. We are just showing the advantages and disadvantages of this extension. For example, the PEAR package, MDB2, has richer functionality of an advanced database abstraction library, which PDO does not.

PDO being a PECL extension, itself relies on database-specific drivers and on other PECL extensions. These drivers must also be installed in order to use PDO (you only need the drivers for the databases you are using). Since the description of installation of PDO and database-specific drivers is beyond the scope of this book, you can refer to PHP manual at `www.php.net/pdo` for technical information regarding installation and upgrade issues.

 PECL is PHP Extension Community Library, a repository of PHP extensions written in C. These extensions offer functionality that would be impossible to implement in PHP, as well as some extensions that exist for performance reasons as the C code is much faster than PHP. The home page of PECL is at `http://pecl.php.net`

Using PDO

As it has been noted in the previous section, PDO is a connection, or data access abstraction library. This means that PDO defines a unified interface for creating and maintaining database connections, issuing queries, quoting parameters, traversing result sets, dealing with prepared statements, and error handling.

We will give a quick overview of these topics here and look at them in greater detail in the following chapters.

Connecting to the Database

Let's consider the well-known MySQL connection scenario:

```
mysql_connect($host, $user, $password);
mysql_select_db($db);
```

Here, we establish a connection and then select the default database for the connection. (We ignore the issue of possible errors.)

In SQLite, for example, we would write something like the following:

```
$dbh = sqlite_open($db, 0666);
```

Here again we ignore errors (we will cover more on this later). For completeness, let's see how we would connect to a PostgreSQL:

pg_connect("host=$host dbname=$db user=$user password=$password");

As you can see, all three databases require quite different ways of opening a connection. While this is not a problem now, but if you always use the same database management system in case you need to migrate, you will have to rewrite your scripts.

Now, let's see what PDO has to offer. As PDO is fully object-oriented, we will be dealing with **connection objects**, and further interaction with the database will involve calling various methods of these objects. The examples above implied the need for something analogous to these connection objects—calls to `mysql_connect` or `pg_connect` return link identifiers and PHP variables of a special type: **resource**. However, we didn't use connection objects then since these two database APIs don't require us to explicitly use them if we only have one connection in our scripts. However, SQLite always requires a link identifier.

With PDO, we will always have to explicitly use the connection object, since there is no other way of calling its methods. (Those unfamiliar with object-oriented programming should refer to Appendix A).

Each of the three above connections could be established in the following manner:

```
// For MySQL:
$conn = new PDO("mysql:host=$host;dbname=$db", $user, $pass);
// For SQLite:
$conn = new PDO("sqlite:$db");
// And for PostgreSQL:
$conn = new PDO("pgsql:host=$host dbname=$db", $user, $pass);
```

As you can see, the only part that is changing here is the first argument passed to the PDO constructor. For SQLite, which does not utilize username and password, the second and third arguments can be skipped.

 SQLite is not a database server, but it is an embedded SQL database library that operates on local files. More information about SQLite can be found at `www.sqlite.org` and more information about using SQLite with PHP can be found at `www.php.net/sqlite`. Information about using SQLite with PDO can be obtained from `www.php.net/manual/en/ref.pdo-sqlite.php`

Connection Strings

As you have seen in previous example, PDO uses the so-called **connection strings** (or Data Source Names, abbreviated to DSN) that allow the PDO constructor to select proper driver and pass subsequent method calls to it. These connection strings or DSNs are different for every database management system and are the only things that you will have to change.

If you are designing a big application that will be able to work with different databases, then this connection string (together with a connection username and a password) can be defined in a configuration file and later used in the following manner (assuming your configuration file is similar to php.ini)

```
$config = parse_ini_file($pathToConfigFile);
$conn = new PDO($config['db.conn'], $config['db.user'],
                $config['db.pass']);
```

Your configuration file might then look like this:

```
db.conn="mysql:host=localhost;dbname=test"
db.user="johns"
db.pass="mypassphrase"
```

We will cover connection strings in more detail in Chapter 2; here we gave a quick example so that you can see how easy it is to connect to different database systems with PDO.

Issuing SQL Queries, Quoting Parameters, and Handling Result Sets

PDO would not be worth a whole book, if it didn't go beyond the single interface for creating database connections. The PDO object introduced in the previous example has all the methods needed to uniformly execute queries regardless of the database used.

Let's consider a simple query that would select all the car make attributes from an imaginary database employed at a used car lot. The query is as simple as the following SQL command:

```
SELECT DISTINCT make FROM cars ORDER BY make;
```

Previously, we would have had to call different functions, depending on the database:

```
// Let's keep our SQL in a single variable
$sql = 'SELECT DISTINCT make FROM cars ORDER BY make';

// Now, assuming MySQL:
mysql_connect('localhost', 'boss', 'password');
mysql_select_db('cars');
$q = mysql_query($sql);

// For SQLite we would do:
```

```
$dbh = sqlite_open('/path/to/cars.ldb', 0666);
$q = sqlite_query($sql, $dbh);

// And for PostgreSQL:
pg_connect("host=localhost dbname=cars user=boss
           password=password");
$q = pg_query($sql);
```

Now that we are using PDO, we can do the following:

```
// assume the $connStr variable holds a valid connection string
// as discussed in previous point
$sql = 'SELECT DISTINCT make FROM cars ORDER BY make';
$conn = new PDO($connStr, 'boss', 'password');
$q = $conn->query($sql);
```

As you can see, doing things the PDO way is not too different from traditional methods of issuing queries. Also, here it should be underlined, that a call to `$conn->query()` is returning another object of class PDOStatement, unlike the calls to `mysql_query()`, `sqlite_query()`, and `pg_query()`, which return PHP variables of the **resource** type.

Now, let's make our simplistic SQL query a bit more complicated so that it selects the total value of all Fords on sale in our imaginary car lot. The query would then look something like this:

```
SELECT sum(price) FROM cars WHERE make='Ford'
```

To make our example even more interesting, let's assume that the name of the car manufacturer is held in a variable ($make) so that we must quote it, before passing it to the database. Our non-PDO queries would now look like this:

```
$make = 'Ford';
// MySQL:
$m = mysql_real_escape_string($make);
$q = mysql_query("SELECT sum(price) FROM cars WHERE make='$m'");

// SQLite:
$m = sqlite_escape_string($make);
$q = sqlite_query("SELECT sum(price) FROM cars WHERE make='$m'",
    $dbh);

// and PostgreSQL:
$m = pg_escape_string($make);
$q = pg_query("SELECT sum(price) FROM cars WHERE make='$m'");
```

The PDO class defines a single method for quoting strings so that they can be used safely in queries. We will discuss security issues such as SQL injection, in Chapter 3. This method does a neat thing; it will automatically add quotes around the value if necessary:

```
$m = $conn->quote($make);
$q = $conn->query("SELECT sum(price) FROM cars WHERE make=$m");
```

Again, you can see that PDO allows you to use the same pattern as you would have used before, but the names of all the methods are unified.

Now that we have issued our query, we will want to see its results. As the query in the last example will always return just one row, we will want more rows. Again, the three databases will require us to call different functions on the $q variable that was returned from one of the three calls to mysql_query(), sqlite_query(), or pg_query(). So our code for getting all the cars will look similar to this:

```
// assume the query is in the $sql variable
$sql = "SELECT DISTINCT make FROM cars ORDER BY make";

// For MySQL:
$q = mysql_query($sql);
while($r = mysql_fetch_assoc($q))
{
   echo $r['make'], "\n";
}

// For SQLite:
$q = sqlite_query($dbh, $sql);
while($r = sqlite_fetch_array($q, SQLITE_ASSOC))
{
   echo $r['make'], "\n";
}

// and, finally, PostgreSQL:
$q = pg_query($sql);
while($r = pg_fetch_assoc($q))
{
   echo $r['make'], "\n";
}
```

As you can see, the idea is the same, but we have to use different function names. Also, note that SQLite requires an extra parameter if we want to get the rows in the same way as with MySQL and PostgreSQL (of course, this could be omitted, but then the returned rows would contain both column name indexed and numerically indexed elements.)

As you may already have guessed, things are pretty straightforward when it comes to PDO: We don't care what the underlying database is, and the methods for fetching rows are the same across all databases. So, the above code could be rewritten for PDO in the following way:

```
$q = $conn->query("SELECT DISTINCT make FROM cars ORDER BY make");
while($r = $q->fetch(PDO::FETCH_ASSOC))
{
   echo $r['make'], "\n";
}
```

Nothing is different from what happens before. One thing to note here is that we explicitly specified the PDO::FETCH_ASSOC fetch style constant here, since PDO's default behavior is to fetch the result rows as arrays indexed both by column name and number. (This behavior is similar to mysql_fetch_array(), sqlite_fetch_array() without the second parameter, or pg_fetch_array().) We will discuss the fetch styles that PDO has to offer in Chapter 2.

The last example was not intended to be used to render HTML pages as it used the newline character to separate lines of output. To use it in a real webpage, you will have to change echo $r['make'], "\n"; to echo $r['make'], "
\n";

Error Handling

Of course, the above examples didn't provide for any error checking, so they are not very useful for real-life applications.

When working with a database, we should check for errors when opening the connection to the database, when selecting the database and after issuing every query. Most web applications, however, just need to display an error message when something goes wrong (without going into error detail, which could reveal some sensitive information). However, when debugging an error, you (as the developer) would need the most detailed error information possible so that you can debug the error in the shortest possible time.

One simplistic scenario would be to abort the script and present the error message (although this is something you probably would not want to do). Depending on the database, our code might look like this:

```
// For SQLite:
$dbh = sqlite_open('/path/to/cars.ldb', 0666) or die
                            ('Error opening SQLite database: ' .
             sqlite_error_string(sqlite_last_error($dbh)));
$q = sqlite_query("SELECT DISTINCT make FROM cars ORDER BY make",
           $dbh) or die('Could not execute query because: ' .
             sqlite_error_string(sqlite_last_error($dbh)));


// and, finally, for PostgreSQL:
pg_connect("host=localhost dbname=cars user=boss
         password=password") or die('Could not connect to
                 PostgreSQL:   .   pg_last_error());
$q = pg_query("SELECT DISTINCT make FROM cars ORDER BY make")
     or die('Could not execute query because: ' . pg_last_error());
```

As you can see, error handling is starting to get a bit different for SQLite compared to MySQL and PostgreSQL. (Note the call to sqlite_error_string (sqlite_last_error($dbh)).)

Before we take a look at how to implement the same error handling strategy with PDO, we should note that this will be only one of the three possible error handling strategies in PDO. We will cover them in detail later in this book. Here we will just use the simplest one:

```
// PDO error handling
// Assume the connection string is one of the following:
// $connStr = 'mysql:host=localhost;dbname=cars'
// $connStr = 'sqlite:/path/to/cars.ldb';
// $connStr = 'pgsql:host=localhost dbname=cars';

try
{
  $conn = new PDO($connStr, 'boss', 'password');
}
catch(PDOException $pe)
{
  die('Could not connect to the database because: ' .
     $pe->getMessage();
}

$q = $conn->query("SELECT DISTINCT make FROM cars ORDER BY make");
```

```
if(!$q)
{
  $ei = $conn->errorInfo();
  die('Could not execute query because: ' . $ei[2]);
}
```

This example shows that PDO will force us to use a slightly different error handling scheme from the traditional one. We wrapped the call to the PDO constructor in a *try ... catch* block. (Those who are new to PHP5's object-oriented features should refer to Appendix A.) This is because while PDO can be instructed not to use exceptions, (in fact, it is PDO's default behavior not to use exceptions), however, you cannot avoid exceptions here. If the call to the constructor fails, an exception will always be thrown.

It is a very good idea to catch that exception because, by default, PHP will abort the script execution and will display an error message like this:

Fatal error: Uncaught exception 'PDOException' with message 'SQLSTATE[28000] [1045] Access denied for user 'bosss'@'localhost' (using password: YES)' in /var/ www/html/pdo.php5:3 Stack trace: #0 c:\www\hosts\localhost\pdo.php5(3): PDO->__construct('mysql:host=loca...', 'bosss', 'password', Array) #1 {main} thrown in /var/www/ html/pdo.php5 on line 3

We made this exception by supplying the wrong username, *bosss*, in the call to the PDO constructor. As you can see from this output, it contains some details that we would not like others to see: Things like file names and script paths, the type of database being used, and most importantly, usernames and passwords. Suppose that this exception had happened when we had supplied the right username and something had gone wrong with the database server. Then the screen output would have contained the real username and password.

If we catch the exception properly, the error output might look like this:

SQLSTATE[28000] [1045] Access denied for user 'bosss'@'localhost' (using password: YES)

This error message contains much less sensitive information. (In fact, this output is very similar to the error output that would be produced by one of our non-PDO examples.) But we will again warn you that the best policy is just show some neutral error message like: "Sorry, the service is temporarily unavailable. Please try again later." Of course, you should also log all errors so that you can find out later whether anything bad has happened.

Prepared Statements

This is a rather advanced topic, but you should become familiar with it. If you are a user of PHP with MySQL or SQLite, then you probably didn't even hear of prepared statements, since PHP's MySQL and SQLite extensions don't offer this functionality. PostgreSQL users might have already used pg_prepare() and pg_execute() in tandem. MySQLi (the *improved* MySQL extension) also offers the prepared statements functionality, but in a somewhat awkward way (despite the possible object-oriented style).

For those who are not familiar with **prepared statements**, we will now give a short explanation.

When developing database-driven, interactive dynamic applications, you will sooner or later need to take user input (which may originate from a form) and pass it as a part of a query to a database. For example, given our cars' database, you might design a feature that will output a list of cars made between any two years. If you allow the user to enter these years in a form, the code will look something like this:

```
// Suppose the years come in the startYear and endYear
// request variables:
$sy = (int)$_REQUEST['startYear'];
$ey = (int)$_REQUEST['endYear'];

if($ey < $sy)
{
  // ensure $sy is less than $ey
  $tmp = $ey;
  $ey = $sy;
  $sy = $tmp;
}

$sql = "SELECT * FROM cars WHERE year >= $sy AND year <= $ey";
// send the query in $sql...
```

In this simple example the query depends on two variables, which are part of the resulting SQL. A corresponding prepared statement in PDO would look something like this:

```
$sql = 'SELECT * FROM cars WHERE year >= ? AND year <= ?';
```

As you can see, we replaced the $sy and $ey variables with **placeholders** in the query body. We can now manipulate this query to create the prepared statement and execute it:

```
// Assuming we have already connected and prepared
// the $sy and $ey variables
$sql = 'SELECT * FROM cars WHERE year >= ? AND year <= ?';
$stmt = $conn->prepare($sql);
$stmt->execute(array($sy, $ey));
```

These three lines of code tells us that the prepared statements are objects (with class PDOStatement). They are created using calls to PDO::prepare() method that accepts an SQL statement with placeholders as its parameters.

The prepared statements then have to be *executed* in order to obtain the query results by calling the PDOStatement::execute() method. As the example shows, we call this method with an array that holds the values for the placeholders. Note how the order of the variables in that array matches the order of the placeholders in the $sql variable. Obviously, the number of elements in the array must be the same as the number of placeholders in the query.

You have probably noticed that we are not saving the result of the call to the PDOStatement::execute() method in any variable. This is because the statement object itself is used to access the query results, so that we can complete our example to look like this:

```
// Suppose the years come in the startYear and endYear
// request variables:
$sy = (int)$_REQUEST['startYear'];
$ey = (int)$_REQUEST['endYear'];

if ($ey < $sy)
{
  // ensure $sy is less than $ey
  $tmp = $ey;
  $ey = $sy;
  $sy = $tmp;
}

$sql = 'SELECT * FROM cars WHERE year >= ? AND year <= ?';
$stmt = $conn->prepare($sql);
$stmt->execute(array($sy, $ey));

// now iterate over the result as if we obtained
// the $stmt in a call to PDO::query()
while ($r = $stmt->fetch(PDO::FETCH_ASSOC))
{
  echo "$r[make] $r[model] $r[year]\n";
}
```

As this complete example shows, we call the PDOStatement::fetch() method until it returns a false value, at which point the loop quits—just like we did in previous examples when discussing result sets traversal.

Of course, the replacement of question mark placeholders with actual values is not the only thing that prepared statements can do. Their power lies in the possibility of being executed as many times as needed. This means that we can call the PDOStatement::execute() method as many times as we want, and every time we can supply different values for the placeholders. For example, we can do this:

```
$sql = 'SELECT * FROM cars WHERE year >= ? AND year <= ?';
$stmt = $conn->prepare($sql);

// Fetch the 'new' cars:
$stmt->execute(array(2005, 2007));
$newCars = $stmt->fetchAll(PDO::FETCH_ASSOC);
// now, 'older' cars:
$stmt->execute(array(2000, 2004));
$olderCars = $stmt->fetchAll(PDO::FETCH_ASSOC);

// Show them
echo 'We have ', count($newCars), ' cars dated 2005-2007';
print_r($newCars);
echo 'Also we have ', count($olderCars), ' cars dated 2000-2004';
print_r($olderCars);
```

Prepared statements tend to execute faster than calls to PDO::query() methods, since the database drivers optimize them only once, in a call to PDO::prepare() methods. Another advantage of using prepared statements is that you don't have to quote the parameters passed in a call to PDOStatement::execute().

In our example we used an explicit cast of the request parameters into integer variables, but we could also have done the following:

```
// Assume we also want to filter by make
$sql = 'SELECT * FROM cars WHERE make=?';
$stmt = $conn->prepare($sql);
$stmt->execute(array($_REQUEST['make']));
```

The prepared statement here will take care of the proper quoting made before executing the query.

And just to finish the introduction of the prepared statements here, probably the best feature about them is that PDO emulates them for every supported database. This means you can use prepared statements with any databases; even if they don't know what they are.

Appropriate Understanding of PDO

Our introduction would not be complete if we didn't mention that. PDO is a database connection abstraction library, and as such, cannot ensure that your code will work for each and every database that it supports. This will only happen if your SQL code is portable. For example, MySQL extends the SQL syntax with this form of insert:

```
INSERT INTO mytable SET x=1, y='two';
```

This kind of SQL code is not portable, as other databases do not understand this way of doing inserts. To ensure that your inserts work across databases, you should replace the above code with :

```
INSERT INTO mytable(x, y) VALUES(1, 'two');
```

This is just one example of incompatibilities that may arise when you use PDO. It is only by making your database schema and SQL portable that can ensure you that your code will be compatible with other databases. However, ensuring this portability is beyond this text.

Summary

This introductory chapter showed you the basics of using PDO when developing dynamic, database-driven applications with the PHP5 language. Also we looked at how PDO can be effectively used to eliminate the differences between different traditional database access APIs and to produce a clearer and more portable code.

In the subsequent chapters, we will be looking at each of the features discussed in this chapter in a greater detail so that you fully master the PHP Data Objects extension.

2
Using PHP Data Objects: First Steps

In the previous chapter, we had a brief overview of what PDO is, how to connect to your favourite database using PDO, how to issue simple queries and how to handle errors. Now that you are convinced that PDO is a good thing and are thinking of using it actively, we will be delving into all the features it has to offer.

In this chapter, we will look more closely at creating connections to a database using PDO and connection strings (data source names), the PDOStatement class, and how to traverse result sets. We will also create a small library management application, which will allow us to manage a collection of books of your home library. The application will be able to list books and authors as well as add and edit them.

We will start by having a look at connection strings, since without them, we will not be able to connect to any database. We will then create a sample database, on which all the examples in this book will be based.

We will depart from the simplistic, imaginary cars' database and create a real working database with several tables. However, now we will be dealing with the classical example of books and authors. We chose this example because such entities are more common. The relational model will be relatively simple, so that you will be able to follow the examples easily, if you have already come across such a database elsewhere.

Connection Strings

Connection strings, or data source names (abbreviated DSN) as they are called in the PDO documentation, are PHP strings that carry such information as the name of the database management system and of the database itself, as well as other connection parameters.

Their advantage over using traditional methods of creating database connection is that you don't have to modify your code if you change the database management system. A connection string can be defined in a configuration file and that file gets processed by your application. Should your database (data source) change, you just edit that configuration file and the rest of your code is kept intact.

The connection strings used in PDO differ due to the existence of different database management systems. However, they always have a common prefix, which denotes the underlying database driver. Remember the MySQL, SQLite, and PostgreSQL examples in the Chapter 1. The three connection strings looked like the following:

```
mysql:host=localhost;dbname=cars
sqlite:/path/to/cars.db
pgsql:host=localhost dbname=cars
```

As we can see, the prefix (the substring before the first semicolon) always keeps the name of the PDO driver. Since we don't have to use different functions to create a connection with PDO, this prefix tells us which internal driver should be used. The rest of the string is parsed by that driver to further initiate the connection. In these cases we supplied the database name; for MySQL and PostgreSQL; we also supplied the host name on which the server runs. (As SQLite is a local database engine, such a parameter would not make sense.)

If you want to specify additional parameters, you should consult your database manual (www.php.net/pdo is always a good place to start). For example, the MySQL PDO driver understands the following parameters:

- **host** - the hostname on which the server runs (*localhost* in our example)
- **port** - the port number where the database server is listening (defaults to *3306*)
- **dbname** - the name of the database (*cars* in our example)
- **unix_socket** - the MySQL UNIX socket (instead of host and/or port).

The SQLite: prefix denotes a connection to a SQLite 3 database. To connect to SQLite 2 database, you have to use SQLite2: prefix. Please see http://www.php.net/manual/en/ref.pdo-sqlite. connection.php for details.

As you might have noticed, different drivers use different character to delimit the parameters—such as a semicolon in MySQL and space in PostgreSQL.

Creating the Sample Database

Suppose that you have a good library at home and you want your computer to help you manage it. You decide to create a web-based database using PHP and, of course, PDO. From now on, the examples will be for MySQL and SQLite databases.

The Data Model

As our database is really simple, we will just have two entities in it: authors and books. Hence, we will be creating two tables with the same names. Now, let's think what properties each of these entities will have.

Authors will have their first name, their last name, and a short biography. The table will need to have a primary key which we will call *id*. We will use it to refer to an author from the books table.

Books are written by authors. (Sometimes they are written by more than one author, but we will consider books written by only one author here.) So we will need a field for the author's ID, as well as the book's title, ISBN number, publisher name, and year of publication. Also, we will include a short summary of what the book is about.

We need for a separate table for authors, because an author might have written more than one book. Also, our example would be really simple otherwise! Thus, we opted for a two-table database structure. If we were to consider books written by more than one author, we would need three tables, which would make the example very complicated.

Creating the MySQL Database

After you have launched your MySQL command line client, you will see the `mysql>` prompt, where you will be able to issue commands to create the database and the tables in it:

```
mysql> create database pdo;
Query OK, 1 row affected (0.05 sec)

mysql> use pdo;
Database changed
mysql> create table books(
    -> id int primary key not null auto_increment,
    -> author int not null,
    -> title varchar(70) not null,
    -> isbn varchar(20),
    -> publisher varchar(30) not null,
    -> year int(4) not null,
    -> summary text(2048));
Query OK, 0 rows affected (0.17 sec)

mysql> create table authors(
    -> id int primary key not null auto_increment,
    -> firstName varchar(30) not null,
    -> lastName varchar(40) not null,
    -> bio text(2048));
Query OK, 0 rows affected (0.00 sec)
```

As you can see, we have created a database and called it pdo. We also created two tables: books and authors, just as we had planned. Now let's see how we do that in SQLite. As we cannot create the database inside the SQLite command line client, we launch it like this:

```
> sqlite3 pdo.db
sqlite> create table books(
   ...> id integer primary key,
   ...> author integer(11) not null,
   ...> title varchar(70) not null,
   ...> isbn varchar(20),
   ...> publisher varchar(30) not null,
   ...> year integer(4) not null,
   ...> summary text(2048));
sqlite> create table authors(
   ...> id integer(11) primary key,
   ...> firstName varchar(30) not null,
   ...> lastName varchar(40) not null,
   ...> bio text(2048));
```

As you can see, the SQL is slightly different for SQLite—the primary keys are declared without the NOT NULL and auto_increment options. In SQLite, a column declared as INTEGER PRIMARY KEY is automatically incremented. Now let's insert some values into our database. The syntax will be the same for MySQL and SQLite so here we will just present the MySQL command line client example. We will start with authors, because we will need their primary key values for inserting into the books table:

```
mysql> insert into authors(firstName, lastName, bio) values(
    -> 'Marc', 'Delisle', 'Marc Delisle is a member of the MySQL
Developers Guide');
Query OK, 1 row affected (0.14 sec)

mysql> insert into authors(firstName, lastName, bio) values(
    -> 'Sohail', 'Salehi', 'In recent years, Sohail has contributed
to over 20 books, mainly in programming and computer graphics');
Query OK, 1 row affected (0.00 sec)

mysql> insert into authors(firstName, lastName, bio) values(
    -> 'Cameron', 'Cooper', 'J. Cameron Cooper has been playing
around on the web since there was not much of a web with which to
play around');
Query OK, 1 row affected (0.00 sec)
```

Now that we have inserted three authors, let's add some books. But before we do, we should know which *author* has which *id*. A simple SELECT query will help us:

```
mysql> select id, firstName, lastName from authors;
+----+-----------+----------+
| id | firstName | lastName |
+----+-----------+----------+
|  1 | Marc      | Delisle  |
|  2 | Sohail    | Salehi   |
|  3 | Cameron   | Cooper   |
+----+-----------+----------+
3 rows in set (0.03 sec)
```

Now we can finally use this information to add three books, each written by one of these authors:

```
mysql> insert into books(author, title, isbn, publisher, year,
summary) values(
    -> 1, 'Creating your MySQL Database: Practical Design Tips and
Techniques', '1904811302', 'Packt Publishing Ltd', '2006',
    -> 'A short guide for everyone on how to structure your data and
set-up your MySQL database tables efficiently and easily.');
```

```
Query OK, 1 row affected (0.00 sec)

mysql> insert into books(author, title, isbn, publisher, year,
summary) values(
    -> 2, 'ImageMagick Tricks', '1904811868', 'Packt Publishing
Ltd', '2006',
    -> 'Unleash the power of ImageMagick with this fast, friendly
tutorial, and tips guide');
Query OK, 1 row affected (0.02 sec)

mysql> insert into books(author, title, isbn, publisher, year,
summary) values(
    -> 3, 'Building Websites with Plone', '1904811027', 'Packt
Publishing Ltd', '2004',
    -> 'An in-depth and comprehensive guide to the Plone content
management system');
Query OK, 1 row affected (0.00 sec)
```

Now that we have filled the `authors` and `books` tables, we may begin to create the first page of our small library management web application.

 The data used is based on real books published by Packt Publishing Ltd (the publisher that brought to you this book you are reading now). To find out more, visit their site at `http://www.packtpub.com`

Designing Our Code

Good application architecture is another key factor of an application, besides the correct data model. As the application that we are going to develop in this chapter, is relatively small, this task is not very complicated. First, we will create two pages that will list books and authors. To begin with, we should think about how these pages would look. To make our simple example small and compact, we will present a header on all pages that will contain links to the books list and the authors list. Later we will add two more pages that will allow us to add an author and a book.

Of course, we should create a common include file that will define the common functions such as the header and footer display and the connection to the database. Our example is really small, so we will not be using any template system or even object-oriented syntax. (Indeed, these topics are beyond the scope of this book.) So, to summarize:

- All common functions (including code to create the PDO connection object) will be kept in an include file (called common.inc.php).

- Every page will be held in a separate file, which includes the common.inc.php file.

- Every page will process data and display it (so that we have no separation of data processing and data presentation, as one would expect from an application designed with the model-view-controller pattern in mind).

Now that we have this small plan, we can begin with our common.inc.php file. As we have just discussed, for now, it will contain the functions to display the header and the footer, as well as the code to create the connection object. Let's keep the PDO object in a global variable called $conn and call our header function showHeader(), and the footer function showFooter(). Also, we will keep the database connection string, user name, and password in this include file:

```php
<?php
/**
 * This is a common include file
 * PDO Library Management example application
 * @author Dennis Popel
 */

// DB connection string and username/password
$connStr = 'mysql:host=localhost;dbname=pdo';
$user = 'root';
$pass = 'root';

/**
 * This function will render the header on every page,
 * including the opening html tag,
 * the head section and the opening body tag.
 * It should be called before any output of the
 * page itself.
 * @param  string $title  the page title
 */
function showHeader($title)
{
  ?>
  <html>
  <head><title><?=htmlspecialchars($title)?></title></head>
  <body>
  <h1><?=htmlspecialchars($title)?></h1>
  <a href="books.php">Books</a>
  <a href="authors.php">Authors</a>
```

```
  <hr>
  <?php
}

/**
 * This function will 'close' the body and html
 * tags opened by the showHeader() function
 */
function showFooter()
{
  ?>
  </body>
  </html>
  <?php
}

// Create the connection object
$conn = new PDO($connStr, $user, $pass);
```

As you can see, the file is really simple, and you will just have to change the values of the $user and $pass variables (on lines 9 and 10) to match your setup. For a SQLite database, you would also have to change line 8 so that it contains an appropriate connection string, for example:

```
$connStr = 'sqlite:/www/hosts/localhost/pdo.db';
```

Of course, you should change this to reflect the path to where you created the SQLite database. Also, the showHeader() function simply renders HTML code and passes the value of the $title variable via the htmlspecialchars() function so that any illegal characters (such as a less-than sign) are properly escaped.

Save the file to your web root directory. This again depends on your web server setup. For example, it could be C:\Apache\htdocs or /var/www/html.

Now, let's create a page that lists the books. We will have to issue the query and then iterate over the results to present each book in its own row. Later, we will create a page that will list all the authors from the database that we created earlier. After we finish this task, we will look at result set traversal.

Let's call our file books.php and create the code:

```
<?php

/**
 * This page lists all the books we have
 * PDO Library Management example application
 * @author Dennis Popel
 */
```

```php
// Don't forget the include
include('common.inc.php');

// Issue the query
$q = $conn->query("SELECT * FROM books ORDER BY title");

// Display the header
showHeader('Books');

// now create the table
?>
<table width="100%" border="1" cellpadding="3">
<tr style="font-weight: bold">
  <td>Title</td>
  <td>ISBN</td>
  <td>Publisher</td>
  <td>Year</td>
  <td>Summary</td>
</tr>

<?php
// Now iterate over every row and display it
while($r = $q->fetch(PDO::FETCH_ASSOC))
{
  ?>
  <tr>
    <td><?=htmlspecialchars($r['title'])?></td>
    <td><?=htmlspecialchars($r['isbn'])?></td>
    <td><?=htmlspecialchars($r['publisher'])?></td>
    <td><?=htmlspecialchars($r['year'])?></td>
    <td><?=htmlspecialchars($r['summary'])?></td>
  </tr>
  <?php
}
?>
</table>

<?php
// Display footer
showFooter();
```

This file should be saved to the directory where the common.inc.php file is located. As you can see, there are more comments and HTML in the code, but there is nothing very complicated here. As we decided earlier, the code includes the common.inc.php file, then renders the page header, issues a query on the line #10, renders the table header, and finally iterates over every row in the result set to output every book's details.

Just as in the first chapter, we traverse the result set in a `while` row, using the `fetch()` method of the `PDOStatement` object (held in the `$q` variable). We instruct this method to return the rows as arrays indexed by table column names (by specifying the `PDO::FETCH_ASSOC` parameter).

Inside the loop, we render the HTML of every row, inserting there the columns from our table. After the loop quits, we close the table and display the footer.

Now it's time to test our first PDO-powered application. Fire up your browser and navigate to `http://localhost/books.php`. If you did everything correctly (so that your web server and database are properly setup), you should see a table similar to the following screenshot (although your page might look much wider, we resized the window before taking a screenshot so that it fits on a printed page):

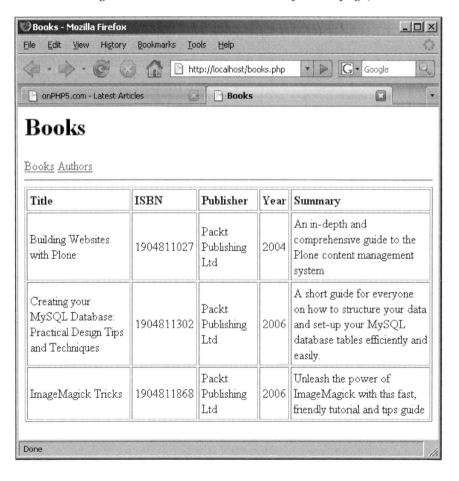

Once we have ensured that our application works with MySQL, let's see how it will work with SQLite. To do this, we have to edit line 8 in the `common.inc.php` file so that it contains the SQLite DSN:

```
$connStr = 'sqlite:/www/hosts/localhost/pdo.db';
```

If you did everything correctly, then after refreshing your browser, you should see the same screen. As we discussed earlier—only one configuration option has to be changed when you start using another database system.

Now, let's create the code for the page that will list the authors. Create a file named `authors.php` and place it in the directory where you saved the previous two files. The code is practically identical to the books listing page:

```php
<?php

/**
 * This page lists all the authors we have
 * PDO Library Management example application
 * @author Dennis Popel
 */

// Don't forget the include
include('common.inc.php');

// Issue the query
$q = $conn->query("SELECT * FROM authors ORDER BY lastName,
                   firstName");

// Display the header
showHeader('Authors');

// now create the table
?>
<table width="100%" border="1" cellpadding="3">
<tr style="font-weight: bold">
  <td>First Name</td>
  <td>Last Name</td>
  <td>Bio</td>
</tr>

<?php
// Now iterate over every row and display it
while($r = $q->fetch(PDO::FETCH_ASSOC))
{
  ?>
  <tr>
    <td><?=htmlspecialchars($r['firstName'])?></td>
    <td><?=htmlspecialchars($r['lastName'])?></td>
```

```
       <td><?=htmlspecialchars($r['bio'])?></td>
    </tr>
    <?php
}
?>
</table>

<?php
// Display footer
showFooter();
```

This file follows the same logic: include the `common.inc.php` file, and then issue the query and traverse the result set. If you have done everything correctly, then you simply click on the **Authors** link located on the books listing page in your browser to get the following page:

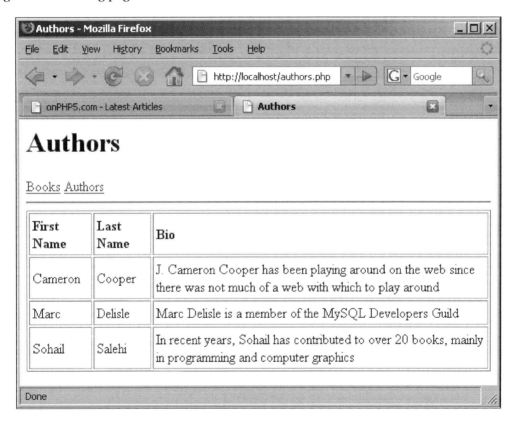

As you can see, the page correctly presents the three authors that we added at the beginning of this chapter. If you want to test this with SQLite, change the line #10 to contain the SQLite connection string. On refreshing your browser, you should see the same page, but now based on the SQLite database contents.

Now that we have created these two pages and seen that using PDO is not complicated, let's look at some theory before we extend the application.

PDO Statements and Result Sets

Our examples made use of two of the main classes in PHP Data Objects: the PDO class, which is used to create a connection and issue queries, and the PDOStatement class, which we use to loop through the result set. We will look at the first of these classes in later chapters. Here, we will examine the PDOStatement class to see what other ways of traversing the result set that it has to offer.

As we already know, instances of the PDOStatement class are returned from the call to PDO::query() method. The main purpose of this class is to provide an interface to the result set. In fact, we have already used its most important method to iterate over the result set. We only looked at one fetch style (or mode of the returned row), but PDO offers several styles. This class can also provide additional information about a result set, such as the number of rows and columns, and fetch the whole result set into a two-dimensional array.

Let's begin by looking at some different fetch styles. We already know the PDO:: FETCH_ASSOC mode that returns an array indexed by column name. The default operation of the PDOStatement object is to return an array indexed by both an integer index and a column name, that is the PDO::FETCH_BOTH fetch mode. We can also request only an integer-indexed array by using the PDO::FETCH_NUM fetch style. PDO also supports fetching rows as objects with the PDO::FETCH_OBJ mode. In this case the call to PDO::fetch() method will return an instance of the stdClass internal class with its properties populated with the row's values. This happens in the following code:

```
$q = $conn->query('SELECT * FROM authors ORDER BY lastName,
                                          firstName');
$r = $q->fetch(PDO::FETCH_OBJ);
var_dump($r);

//would print:
object(stdClass)#4 (4)
{
  ["id"]=>
  string(1) "3"
  ["firstName"]=>
  string(7) "Cameron"
  ["lastName"]=>
  string(6) "Cooper"
  ["bio"]=>
```

```
string(112) "J. Cameron Cooper has been playing around on the web
since there was not much of a web with which to play around"
}
```

The `PDOStatement` class also allows you to set the fetch mode once for all subsequent calls to its `fetch()` method. This is done via the `PDOStatement::setFetchMode()` method, which accepts any of the `PDO::FETCH_ASSOC`, `PDO::FETCH_BOTH`, `PDO::FETCH_NUM`, and `PDO::FETCH_OBJ` constants. With this in mind, we can rewrite lines 23 and 24 of the `authors.php` file to look like this:

```
// Now iterate over every row and display it
$q->setFetchMode(PDO::FETCH_ASSOC);
while($r = $q->fetch())
{
```

You can try it on your copy of the `authors.php` file and refresh the browser to see that this works.

You may have noticed that the SQLite, MySQL, and pgSQL PHP extensions all offer similar functionality. Indeed, we can use any of the `mysql_fetch_row()`, `mysql_fetch_assoc()`, `mysql_fetch_array()`, or `mysql_fetch_object()` functions to achieve the same effect. That's why PDO goes further and enables us to use three additional fetch modes. These three modes can be only set via `PDOStatement::setFetchMode()` call, and here they are:

- PDO::FETCH_COLUMN allows you to instruct the `PDOStatement` object to return the specified column of every row. In this case, `PDO::fetch()` will return a scalar value. The columns are numbered starting with 0. This happens in the following code snippet:

```
$q = $conn->query('SELECT * FROM authors ORDER BY lastName,
    firstName');
$q->setFetchMode(PDO::FETCH_COLUMN, 1);
while($r = $q->fetch())
{
  var_dump($r);
}
//would print:
string(7) "Cameron"
string(4) "Marc"
string(6) "Sohail"
```

This reveals that the call to `$q->fetch()` does indeed returns scalar values (not arrays). Note that the column with the index 1 should be the author's last name, not their first name, if you are simply looking at the page with authors list. However, our query looks like SELECT * FROM authors, so it also retrieves the author ids, which are stored into the 0th column. You should be aware of this, as you may spend hours looking for the source of such a logical error.

- PDO::FETCH_INTO can be used to modify an instance of an object. Let's rewrite our above example as follows:

```
$q = $conn->query('SELECT * FROM authors ORDER BY lastName,
                                            firstName');
$r = new stdClass();
$q->setFetchMode(PDO::FETCH_INTO, $r);
while($q->fetch())
{
  var_dump($r);
}
//would print something like:
object(stdClass)#3 (4)
{
  ["id"]=>
  string(1) "3"
  ["firstName"]=>
  string(7) "Cameron"
  ["lastName"]=>
  string(6) "Cooper"
  ["bio"]=>
  string(112) "J. Cameron Cooper has been playing around on the
  web since there was not much of a web with which to play around"
}
object(stdClass)#3 (4)
{
  ["id"]=>
  string(1) "1"
  ["firstName"]=>
  string(4) "Marc"
  ["lastName"]=>
  string(7) "Delisle"
  ["bio"]=>
  string(54) "Marc Delisle is a member of the MySQL Developer
             Guide"
}
object(stdClass)#3 (4)
```

```
{
  ["id"]=>
  string(1) "2"
  ["firstName"]=>
  string(6) "Sohail"
  ["lastName"]=>
  string(6) "Salehi"
  ["bio"]=>
  string(101) "In recent years, Sohail has contributed to over 20
  books, mainly in programming and computer graphics"
}
```

Inside the `while` loop we didn't assign the $r variable, which is the return value of $q->fetch(). $r has been bound to this method via the call to $q->setFetchMode() before the loop.

- PDO::FETCH_CLASS can be used to return objects of a specified class. For every row, an instance of this class will be created with the properties named and assigned the values of the result set columns. Note that the class does not necessarily have these properties declared since PHP allows runtime creation of object properties. For example:

```
$q = $conn->query('SELECT * FROM authors ORDER BY lastName,
                                             firstName');
$q->setFetchMode(PDO::FETCH_CLASS, stdClass);
while($r = $q->fetch())
{
  var_dump($r);
}
```

This will print output similar to that for the previous example. Also, this fetch mode allows you to create instances by passing an array of parameters to their constructors:

```
$q->setFetchMode(PDO::FETCH_CLASS, SomeClass, array(1, 2, 3));
```

(This will work only if the SomeClass class has been defined.)

We would recommend using PDOStatement::setFetchMode() as it is more convenient and easier to maintain (and, of course, has more features).

Describing all of these fetch modes may seem excessive, but each of them is useful in certain situations. Indeed, you may have noticed that the list of books is somewhat incomplete. It does not contain the author's name. We will add this missing column, and to make our example trickier, we will make the author's name clickable and link it to the author's profile page (which we will create). This profile page needs the author's ID so that we can pass it in the URL. It will display all the information that we have about the author, as well as the list of all of their books. Let's begin with this author's profile page:

```php
<?php
/**
 * This page shows an author's profile
 * PDO Library Management example application
 * @author Dennis Popel
 */

// Don't forget the include
include('common.inc.php');

// Get the author
$id = (int)$_REQUEST['id'];
$q = $conn->query("SELECT * FROM authors WHERE id=$id");
$author = $q->fetch(PDO::FETCH_ASSOC);
$q->closeCursor();

// Now see if the author is valid - if it's not,
// we have an invalid ID
if(!$author) {
  showHeader('Error');
  echo "Invalid Author ID supplied";
  showFooter();
  exit;
}

// Display the header - we have no error
showHeader("Author: $author[firstName] $author[lastName]");

// Now fetch all his books
$q = $conn->query("SELECT * FROM books WHERE author=$id ORDER
                                          BY title");
$q->setFetchMode(PDO::FETCH_ASSOC);
// now display everything
?>
<h2>Author</h2>
<table width="60%" border="1" cellpadding="3">
<tr>
  <td><b>First Name</b></td>
```

```
    <td><?=htmlspecialchars($author['firstName'])?></td>
  </tr>
  <tr>
    <td><b>Last Name</b></td>
    <td><?=htmlspecialchars($author['lastName'])?></td>
  </tr>
  <tr>
    <td><b>Bio</b></td>
    <td><?=htmlspecialchars($author['bio'])?></td>
  </tr>
  </table>

  <h2>Books</h2>
  <table width="100%" border="1" cellpadding="3">
  <tr style="font-weight: bold">
    <td>Title</td>
    <td>ISBN</td>
    <td>Publisher</td>
    <td>Year</td>
    <td>Summary</td>
  </tr>
  <?php
  // Now iterate over every book and display it
  while($r = $q->fetch())
  {
    ?>
    <tr>
      <td><?=htmlspecialchars($r['title'])?></td>
      <td><?=htmlspecialchars($r['isbn'])?></td>
      <td><?=htmlspecialchars($r['publisher'])?></td>
      <td><?=htmlspecialchars($r['year'])?></td>
      <td><?=htmlspecialchars($r['summary'])?></td>
    </tr>
    <?php
  }
  ?>
  </table>

  <?php
  // Display footer
  showFooter();
```

Name this file `author.php` and save it to the directory where rest of the files are located.

Here are a few comments about the code:

- We handle the author's ID (line #13) by explicitly casting it to an integer so as to prevent a possible security hole. We later pass the $id variable to the text of the query without quoting as it's OK to do so with numeric values.

- We will discuss the call to `$q->closeCursor();  $q = null` on line #13 in the following chapters. Here we will just note that it's a good idea to call this method between queries executed on the same connection object and then set it to null. Our example would not work without it. Also note that we don't need this after the last query.

- We also do simple error handling here: we check whether the author ID is invalid. If it is invalid, we display an error message and then exit. (See lines 22 to 27.)

- On lines 25 and 27, we use the author's ID to create the query and set the fetch mode to be `PDO::FETCH_ASSOC`. Then we proceed to the display of data: first we render the author's details and then all his books.

Now you can return to your browser and point it to the URL: `http://localhost/author.php?id=1`.

The following screen should appear:

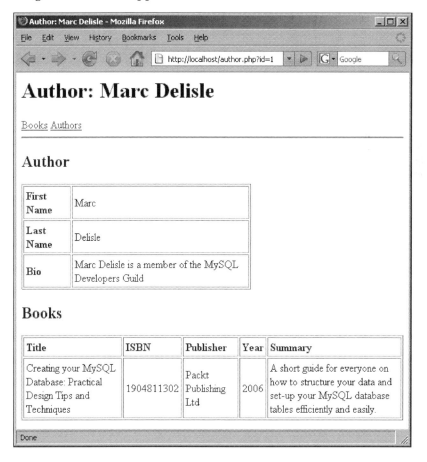

As you can see, everything is correct on the page: The author's details, which we filed first (`id=1`), and the only book by this author. Now let's see how our application reacts to an invalid ID submitted. We know that we have only three authors, so any number other than 1, 2, or 3 is invalid. Also, a non-number parameter will evaluate to 0, which is invalid. If we change the URL in the address bar to `http://localhost/author.php?id=zzz`. We will end up with the following:

You should also switch to SQLite in `common.inc.php` and see that this page also works with this database.

Now, let's modify our existing `books.php` file to add an author column with a link to the author's profile page. We will have to join the two tables where the book's `author` field equals the author's ID field, and select the author's ID, first name, and last name. So our query will look like this:

```
SELECT authors.id, authors.firstName, authors.lastName, books.* FROM
authors, books WHERE author=authors.id ORDER BY title;
```

Before we proceed with the changes, let's run this query in the command line client. We will also modify this query for the client as its window will not fit the whole row:

```
mysql> SELECT authors.id, firstName, lastName, books.id, title FROM
authors, books WHERE books.author=authors.id;
+----+-----------+----------+----+----------------------------+
| id | firstName | lastName | id | title                      |
+----+-----------+----------+----+----------------------------+
|  1 | Marc      | Delisle  |  1 | Creating your MySQL...     |
|  2 | Sohail    | Salehi   |  2 | ImageMagick Tricks         |
|  3 | Cameron   | Cooper   |  3 | Building Websites with Plone |
+----+-----------+----------+----+----------------------------+
3 rows in set (0.00 sec)
```

As you can see, the query is returning two columns called id. This means that we will not be able to use the PDO::FETCH_ASSOC mode, since there can be only id array index. Here we have two options: Either use the PDO::FETCH_NUM mode or retrieve the ID fields using aliases.

Let's see how we would code the page using PDO::FETCH_NUM:

```php
<?php
/**
 * This page lists all the books we have
 * PDO Library Management example application
 * @author Dennis Popel
 */

// Don't forget the include
include('common.inc.php');

// Issue the query
$q = $conn->query("SELECT authors.id, firstName, lastName, books.*
                   FROM authors, books WHERE author=authors.id ORDER
                   BY title");
$q->setFetchMode(PDO::FETCH_NUM);

// Display the header
showHeader('Books');

// now create the table
?>
<table width="100%" border="1" cellpadding="3">
<tr style="font-weight: bold">
  <td>Author</td>
  <td>Title</td>
  <td>ISBN</td>
  <td>Publisher</td>
  <td>Year</td>
  <td>Summary</td>
</tr>

<?php
// Now iterate over every row and display it
while($r = $q->fetch())
{
  ?>
  <tr>
    <td><a href="author.php?id=<?=$r[0]?>">
    <?=htmlspecialchars("$r[1] $r[2]")?></a></td>
    <td><?=htmlspecialchars($r[5])?></td>
    <td><?=htmlspecialchars($r[6])?></td>
    <td><?=htmlspecialchars($r[7])?></td>
    <td><?=htmlspecialchars($r[8])?></td>
```

```
     <td><?=htmlspecialchars($r[9])?></td>
   </tr>
   <?php
}
?>
</table>

<?php
// Display footer
showFooter();
```

Note the highlighted lines—they contain the changes; the rest of file is the same. As you can see, we added the call to `$q->setFetchMode()` and changed the loop to use numeric column indexes.

If we navigate back to `http://localhost/books.php`, we will see a list similar to the one in this screenshot:

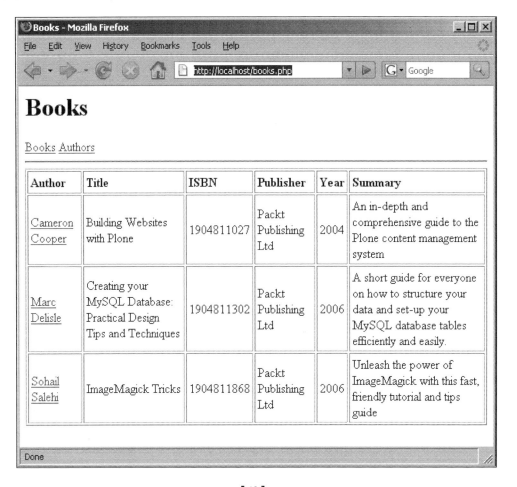

We can click on every author to get to their profile page. Of course, changing back to SQLite in `common.inc.php` should also work.

Another (and much better) option is to use aliases for column names in the SQL code. If we do this, we will not have to take care of the numeric indexes and change the code every time we add or remove columns from our tables. We just change the SQL to the following:

```
SELECT authors.id AS authorId, firstName, lastName, books.* FROM
        authors, books WHERE author=authors.id ORDER BY title;
```

The final version of `books.php` will look like this:

```php
<?php
/**
 * This page lists all the books we have
 * PDO Library Management example application
 * @author Dennis Popel
 */

// Don't forget the include
include('common.inc.php');

// Issue the query
$q = $conn->query("SELECT authors.id AS authorId, firstName,
                    lastName, books.* FROM authors, books WHERE
                    author=authors.id
                    ORDER BY title");
$q->setFetchMode(PDO::FETCH_ASSOC);

// Display the header
showHeader('Books');

// now create the table
?>
<table width="100%" border="1" cellpadding="3">
<tr style="font-weight: bold">
  <td>Author</td>
  <td>Title</td>
  <td>ISBN</td>
  <td>Publisher</td>
  <td>Year</td>
  <td>Summary</td>
</tr>

<?php
// Now iterate over every row and display it
while($r = $q->fetch())
```

```
{
  ?>
  <tr>
    <td><a href="author.php?id=<?=$r['authorId']?>">
    <?=htmlspecialchars("$r[firstName] $r[lastName]")?></a></td>
    <td><?=htmlspecialchars($r['title'])?></td>
    <td><?=htmlspecialchars($r['isbn'])?></td>
    <td><?=htmlspecialchars($r['publisher'])?></td>
    <td><?=htmlspecialchars($r['year'])?></td>
    <td><?=htmlspecialchars($r['summary'])?></td>
  </tr>
  <?php
}
?>
</table>

<?php
// Display footer
showFooter();
```

Note that we changed the fetch mode back to `PDO::FETCH_ASSOC`. Also, we access the author's ID on line 34 with `$r['authorId']`, since we aliased that column with `authorId` in the query.

PDO also allows us to fetch all the results into an array. We may need this for further processing or for passing to some function. However, this should be done only for small result sets. This is highly discouraged for applications like ours, because we simply display the list of books or authors. Fetching a big result set into an array will require memory allocated for the whole result, while in our case we display results row by row, so this requires memory for just one row.

This method is called `PDOStatement::fetchAll()`. The resulting array is either a two-dimensional array or a list of objects—this depends on the fetch mode. This method accepts all the `PDO::FETCH_xxxx` constants, just like `PDOStatement::fetch()`. For example, we could rewrite our `books.php` file in the following manner to achieve the same result. Here is the relevant part of `books.php` lines 9 to 46:

```
// Issue the query
$q = $conn->query("SELECT authors.id AS authorId, firstName,
                   lastName, books.* FROM authors, books WHERE
                   author=authors.id ORDER BY title");
$books = $q->fetchAll(PDO::FETCH_ASSOC);

// Display the header
```

```php
showHeader('Books');
// now create the table
?>
<table width="100%" border="1" cellpadding="3">
<tr style="font-weight: bold">
  <td>Author</td>
  <td>Title</td>
  <td>ISBN</td>
  <td>Publisher</td>
  <td>Year</td>
  <td>Summary</td>
</tr>

<?php
// Now iterate over every row and display it
foreach($books as $r)
{
  ?>
  <tr>
    <td><a href="author.php?id=<?=$r['authorId']?>">
    <?=htmlspecialchars("$r[firstName] $r[lastName]")?></a></td>
    <td><?=htmlspecialchars($r['title'])?></td>
    <td><?=htmlspecialchars($r['isbn'])?></td>
    <td><?=htmlspecialchars($r['publisher'])?></td>
    <td><?=htmlspecialchars($r['year'])?></td>
    <td><?=htmlspecialchars($r['summary'])?></td>
  </tr>
  <?php
}
?>
</table>
```

Note the highlighted lines here—we fetch the whole result into the `$books` array on line 5 and then iterate over it with a `foreach` loop on line 21. If you run the modified page, you will see that we receive the same result. This will also work if we change to SQLite database in the `common.inc.php` file.

The `PDOStatement::fetchAll()` method also allows us to select the values of a single column with the `PDO::FETCH_COLUMN` mode. If we want to fetch the entire book titles using the query from the last example, we can do the following (note the number and ordering of columns):

```php
$q = $conn->query("SELECT authors.id AS authorId, firstName,
                lastName, books.* FROM authors, books WHERE
                author=authors.id ORDER BY title");
$books = $q->fetchAll(PDO::FETCH_COLUMN, 5);
var_dump($books);
```

This would give the following output:

```
array(3)
{
  [0]=>
  string(28) "Building Websites with Plone"
  [1]=>
  string(66) "Creating your MySQL Database: Practical Design Tips and
              Techniques"
  [2]=>
  string(18) "ImageMagick Tricks"
}
```

As you can see, when a single column is requested, this method returns one-dimensional array.

Retrieving Result Set Metadata

As we have seen in the previous section, the PDOStatement class allows us to retrieve some information about the data contained in the result set. This information is called **metadata**, and you probably have already used some of it one way or another.

The most important metadata about a result set is, of course, the number of rows it contains. We can use the row count to enhance user experience by, for example, paginating long result sets. Our example library application is still quite small, with only three books so far, but as our database grows, we surely will need some tools to get the total row count for every table displayed and paginate it for easy browsing.

Traditionally, you would use the mysql_num_rows(), sqlite_num_rows() function or the pg_num_rows() function (depending on your database) to get the total number of rows returned by the query. In PDO, the method responsible for retrieving the number of rows is called PDOStatement::rowCount(). However, if you want to test it with the following code:

```
$q = $conn->query("SELECT * FROM books ORDER BY title");
$q->setFetchMode(PDO::FETCH_ASSOC);
var_dump($q->rowCount());
```

you will see that PDO returns 0 both for MySQL and SQLite. This is because PDO operates differently from the traditional database extensions. The documentation says, "If the last SQL statement executed by the associated PDOStatement class was a SELECT statement, some databases may return the number of rows returned by that statement. However, this behavior is not guaranteed for all databases and should not be relied on for portable applications." Neither MySQL nor SQLite drivers support this functionality, and that's why the return value of this method is 0. We will see how to count the number of rows returned with PDO (so that this is a really portable method) in Chapter 5.

> A *RDBMS* does not know how many rows a query will return till the last row has been retrieved. This is done because of performance considerations. In most cases, queries with a WHERE clause, return only part of the rows stored in a table, and database servers do their best to ensure that such queries execute as fast as possible. This means that they start returning rows as soon as they discover those that match the WHERE clause—this happens much earlier than when the last row is reached. That is why they really don't know how many rows will be returned beforehand. The mysql_num_rows(), sqlite_num_rows() function or the pg_num_rows() function operates on result sets that have been prefetched into memory (buffered queries). PDO's default behavior is to use unbuffered queries. We will speak about MySQL buffered queries later in Chapter 6.

Another method that can be of interest is the PDOStatement::columnCount() method, which returns the number of columns in the result set. It is handy when we execute arbitrary queries. (For example, a database management application like phpMyAdmin could make great use of this method, as it allows a user to type arbitrary SQL queries.) We can use it in the following way:

```
$q = $conn->query("SELECT authors.id AS authorId, firstName,
                 lastName, books.* FROM authors, books WHERE
                  author=authors.id ORDER BY title");
var_dump($q->columnCount());
```

This will reveal that our query returns a result set containing 10 columns (seven columns from the **books** table and three columns from **authors** table).

Unfortunately, PDO currently does not allow you to retrieve the name of the table or of a particular column from a result set to which it belongs. This functionality is useful if your application utilizes queries that join two or more tables. In such case, it is possible to fetch the table name for every column given its numeric index, starting with 0. However, proper use of column aliases eliminates the need to use such functionality. For example, when we modified the books listing page to display the author's name, we aliased the author's ID column to avoid name conflict. That alias clearly identifies the column as belonging to the authors table.

Summary

In this chapter, we took our first steps with PDO and even created a small working database-driven, dynamic application that runs on two different databases. Now you should be able to connect to any supporting database, using the rules for constructing a connection string. You should then be able to run queries against it, and to traverse and display the result set.

In the next chapter, we will deal with a very important aspect of any database-driven application—error handling. We will also extend our example application by giving it the ability to add and edit books and authors, thus making it more realistic and useful.

3
Error Handling

Now that we have built our first application that uses PDO, we will take a closer look at an important aspect of user-friendly web applications—error handling. Not only does it inform the user about an error condition, it also limits the damage if an error is not detected when it occurred.

Most web applications have rather simple error handling strategy. When an error occurs, the script terminates and an error page is presented. The error should be logged in the error log, and the developers or maintainers should check the logs periodically. The most common sources of errors in database-driven web applications are the following:

- Server software failure or overload such as the famous "too many connections" error

- Inappropriate configuration of the application, which may happen when we use an incorrect connection string, a rather common mistake when an application is moved from one host to another

- Improper validation of user input, which may lead to malformed SQL and subsequent failure of the query

- Inserting a record with a duplicate primary key or unique index value, which either results from an error in the business logic of the application or may occur in a controlled situation

- Syntax errors in SQL statements

In this chapter, we will extend our application so that we can edit existing records as well as add new records. As we will deal with user input supplied via web forms, we have to take care of its validation. Also, we may add error handling so that we can react to non-standard situations and present the user with a friendly message.

Before we proceed, let's briefly examine the sources of errors mentioned above and see what error handling strategy should be applied in each case. Our error handling strategy will use exceptions, so you should be familiar with them. If you are not, you can refer to Appendix A, which will introduce you to the new object-oriented features of PHP5.

We have consciously chosen to use exceptions, even though PDO can be instructed not to use them, because there is one situation where they cannot be avoided. The PDO constructors always throw an exception when the database object cannot be created, so we may as well use exceptions as our main error-trapping method throughout the code.

Sources of Errors

To create an error handling strategy, we should first analyze where errors can happen. Errors can happen on every call to the database, and although this is rather unlikely, we will look at this scenario. But before doing so, let's check each of the possible error sources and define a strategy for dealing with them.

Server Software Failure or Overload

This can happen on a really busy server, which cannot handle any more incoming connections. For example, there may be a lengthy update running in the background. The outcome is that we are unable to get any data from the database, so we should do the following.

If the PDO constructor fails, we present a page displaying a message, which says that the user's request could not be fulfilled at this time and that they should try again later. Of course, we should also log this error because it may require immediate attention. (A good idea would be emailing the database administrator about the error.)

The problem with this error is that, while it usually manifests itself before a connection is established with the database (in a call to PDO constructor), there is a small risk that it can happen after the connection has been established (on a call to a method of the PDO or PDOStatement object when the database server is being shutdown). In this case, our reaction will be the same—present the user with an error message asking them to try again later.

Improper Configuration of the Application

This error can only occur when we move the application across servers where database access details differ; this may be when we are uploading from a development server to production server, where database setups differ. This is not an error that can happen during normal execution of the application, but care should be taken while uploading as this may interrupt the site's operation.

If this error occurs, we can display another error message like: "This site is under maintenance". In this scenario, the site maintainer should react immediately, as without correcting, the connection string the application cannot normally operate.

Improper Validation of User Input

This is an error which is closely related to SQL injection vulnerability. Every developer of database-driven applications must undertake proper measures to validate and filter all user inputs. This error may lead to two major consequences: Either the query will fail due to malformed SQL (so that nothing particularly bad happens), or an SQL injection may occur and application security may be compromised. While their consequences differ, both these problems can be prevented in the same way.

Let's consider the following scenario. We accept some numeric value from a form and insert it into the database. To keep our example simple, assume that we want to update a book's year of publication. To achieve this, we can create a form that has two fields: A hidden field containing the book's ID, and a text field to enter the year. We will skip implementation details here, and see how using a poorly designed script to process this form could lead to errors and put the whole system at risk.

The form processing script will examine two request variables: $_REQUEST['book'], which holds the book's ID and $_REQUEST['year'], which holds the year of publication. If there is no validation of these values, the final code will look similar to this:

```
$book = $_REQUEST['book'];
$year = $_REQUEST['year'];
$sql = "UPDATE books SET year=$year WHERE id=$book";
$conn->query($sql);
```

Let's see what happens if the user leaves the book field empty. The final SQL would then look like:

```
UPDATE books SET year= WHERE id=1;
```

This SQL is malformed and will lead to a syntax error. Therefore, we should ensure that both variables are holding numeric values. If they don't, we should redisplay the form with an error message.

Now, let's see how an attacker might exploit this to delete the contents of the entire table. To achieve this, they could just enter the following into the `year` field:

```
2007; DELETE FROM books;
```

This turns a single query into three queries:

```
UPDATE books SET year=2007; DELETE FROM books; WHERE book=1;
```

Of course, the third query is malformed, but the first and second will execute, and the database server will report an error. To counter this problem, we could use simple validation to ensure that the `year` field contains four digits. However, if we have text fields, which can contain arbitrary characters, the field's values must be escaped prior to creating the SQL.

Inserting a Record with a Duplicate Primary Key or Unique Index Value

This problem may happen when the application is inserting a record with duplicate values for the primary key or a unique index. For example, in our database of authors and books, we might want to prevent the user from entering the same book twice by mistake. To do this, we can create a unique index of the ISBN column of the `books` table. As every book has a unique ISBN, any attempt to insert the same ISBN will generate an error. We can trap this error and react accordingly, by displaying an error message asking the user to correct the ISBN or cancel its addition.

Syntax Errors in SQL Statements

This error may occur if we haven't properly tested the application. A good application must not contain these errors, and it is the responsibility of the development team to test every possible situation and check that every SQL statement performs without syntax errors.

If this type of an error occurs, then we trap it with exceptions and display a fatal error message. The developers must correct the situation at once.

Now that we have learned a bit about possible sources of errors, let's examine how PDO handles errors.

Types of Error Handling in PDO

By default, PDO uses the **silent error handling mode**. This means that any error that arises when calling methods of the PDO or PDOStatement classes go unreported. With this mode, one would have to call PDO::errorInfo(), PDO::errorCode(), PDOStatement::errorInfo(), or PDOStatement::errorCode(), every time an error occurred to see if it really did occur. Note that this mode is similar to traditional database access—usually, the code calls mysql_errno() and mysql_error() (or equivalent functions for other database systems) after calling functions that could cause an error, after connecting to a database and after issuing a query.

Another mode is the **warning mode**. Here, PDO will act identical to the traditional database access. Any error that happens during communication with the database would raise an E_WARNING error. Depending on the configuration, an error message could be displayed or logged into a file.

Finally, PDO introduces a modern way of handling database connection errors—by using **exceptions**. Every failed call to any of the PDO or PDOStatement methods will throw an exception.

As we have previously noted, PDO uses the silent mode, by default. To switch to a desired error handling mode, we have to specify it by calling PDO::setAttribute() method. Each of the error handling modes is specified by the following constants, which are defined in the PDO class:

- PDO::ERRMODE_SILENT – the *silent* strategy.
- PDO::ERRMODE_WARNING – the *warning* strategy.
- PDO::ERRMODE_EXCEPTION – use *exceptions.*

To set the desired error handling mode, we have to set the PDO::ATTR_ERRMODE attribute in the following way:

```
$conn->setAttribute(PDO::ATTR_ERRMODE, PDO::ERRMODE_EXCEPTION);
```

To see how PDO throws an exception, edit the common.inc.php file by adding the above statement after the line #46. If you want to test what will happen when PDO throws an exception, change the connection string to specify a nonexistent database. Now point your browser to the books listing page.

You should see an output similar to:

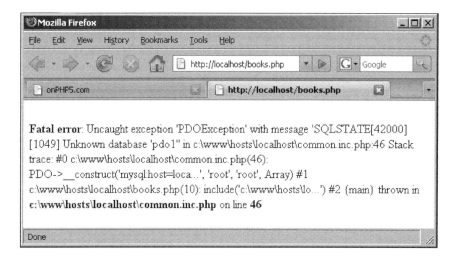

This is PHP's default reaction to uncaught exceptions—they are regarded as fatal errors and program execution stops. The error message reveals the class of the exception, PDOException, the error description, and some debug information, including name and line number of the statement that threw the exception. Note that if you want to test SQLite, specifying a non-existent database may not work as the database will get created if it does not exist already. To see that it does work for SQLite, change the $connStr variable on line 10 so that there is an illegal character in the database name:

```
$connStr = 'sqlite:/path/to/pdo*.db';
```

Refresh your browser and you should see something like this:

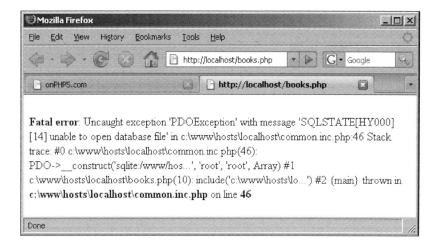

As you can see, a message similar to the previous example is displayed, specifying the cause and the location of the error in the source code.

Defining an Error Handling Function

If we know that a certain statement or block of code can throw an exception, we should wrap that code within the *try...catch* block to prevent the default error message being displayed and present a user-friendly error page. But before we proceed, let's create a function that will render an error message and exit the application. As we will be calling it from different script files, the best place for this function is, of course, the `common.inc.php` file.

Our function, called `showError()`, will do the following:

- Render a heading saying "Error".

- Render the error message. We will escape the text with the `htmlspecialchars()` function and process it with the `nl2br()` function so that we can display multi-line messages. (This function will convert all line break characters to `<br>` tags.)

- Call the `showFooter()` function to close the opening `<html>` and `<body>` tags. The function will assume that the application has already called the `showHeader()` function. (Otherwise, we will end up with broken HTML.)

We will also have to modify the block that creates the connection object in `common.inc.php` to catch the possible exception. With all these changes, the new version of `common.inc.php` will look like this:

```php
<?php

/**
 * This is a common include file
 * PDO Library Management example application
 * @author Dennis Popel
 */

// DB connection string and username/password
$connStr = 'mysql:host=localhost;dbname=pdo';
$user = 'root';
$pass = 'root';

/**
 * This function will render the header on every page,
 * including the opening html tag,
 * the head section and the opening body tag.
 * It should be called before any output of the
```

```php
 * page itself.
 * @param  string $title  the page title
 */
function showHeader($title)
{
  ?>
  <html>
    <head><title><?=htmlspecialchars($title)?></title></head>
    <body>
    <h1><?=htmlspecialchars($title)?></h1>
    <a href="books.php">Books</a>
    <a href="authors.php">Authors</a>
  <hr>
  <?php
}

/**
 * This function will 'close' the body and html
 * tags opened by the showHeader() function
 */
function showFooter()
{
  ?>
  </body>
  </html>
  <?php
}

/**
 * This function will display an error message, call the
 * showFooter() function and terminate the application
 * @param  string $message  the error message
 */
function showError($message)
{
  echo "<h2>Error</h2>";
  echo nl2br(htmlspecialchars($message));
  showFooter();
  exit();
}

// Create the connection object
try
{
  $conn = new PDO($connStr, $user, $pass);
```

```
    $conn->setAttribute(PDO::ATTR_ERRMODE, PDO::ERRMODE_EXCEPTION);
}
catch(PDOException $e)
{
    showHeader('Error');
    showError("Sorry, an error has occurred. Please try your request
                later\n" . $e->getMessage());
}
```

As you can see, the newly created function is pretty straightforward. The more interesting part is the *try...catch* block that we use to trap the exception. Now with these modifications we can test how a real exception will get processed. To do that, make sure your connection string is wrong (so that it specifies wrong database name for MySQL or contains invalid file name for SQLite). Point your browser to books.php and you should see the following window:

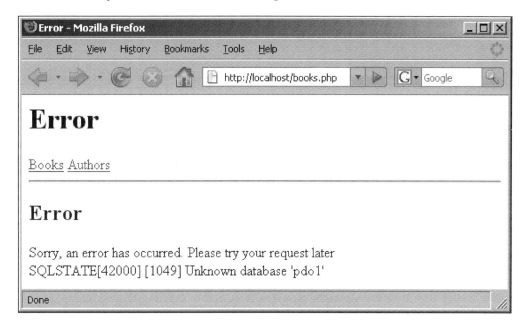

Creating the Edit Book Page

As we have discussed earlier, we want to extend our application so that we can add and edit books and authors. Also, our system should be able to protect us from entering the same book twice—by enforcing the unique index on the ISBN column in the books table.

Before we proceed with the code, we will create the index. Fire up your command line client and enter the following command (which is the same for MySQL and SQLite):

```
CREATE UNIQUE INDEX idx_isbn ON books(isbn);
```

We will also make our edit book page serve two purposes at once—adding a new book and editing an existing one. The script will distinguish which action to take by the presence of the book ID, either in an URL or in a hidden form field. We will link to this new page from within books.php, so that we will be able to edit every book just by clicking on a link on the books listing page.

This page is more complicated than those described in the previous chapter, so I will provide you with the code first and then discuss it. Let's call this page edit Book.php:

```php
<?php

/**
 * This page allows to add or edit a book
 * PDO Library Management example application
 * @author Dennis Popel
 */

// Don't forget the include
include('common.inc.php');

// See if we have the book ID passed in the request
$id = (int)$_REQUEST['book'];
if($id) {
  // We have the ID, get the book details from the table
  $q = $conn->query("SELECT * FROM books WHERE id=$id");
  $book = $q->fetch(PDO::FETCH_ASSOC);
  $q->closeCursor();
  $q = null;
}
else {
  // We are creating a new book
  $book = array();
}

// Now get the list of all authors' first and last names
// We will need it to create the dropdown box for author
$authors = array();
$q = $conn->query("SELECT id, lastName, firstName FROM authors ORDER
                                        BY lastName, firstName");
$q->setFetchMode(PDO::FETCH_ASSOC);
while($a = $q->fetch())
{
  $authors[$a['id']] = "$a[lastName], $a[firstName]";
}
```

```
// Now see if the form was submitted
if($_POST['submit']) {
  // Validate every field
  $warnings = array();
  // Title should be non-empty
  if(!$_POST['title'])
{
    $warnings[] = 'Please enter book title';
}
  // Author should be a key in the $authors array
  if(!array_key_exists($_POST['author'], $authors))
  {
    $warnings[] = 'Please select author for the book';
  }
  // ISBN should be a 10-digit number
  if(!preg_match('~^\d{10}$~', $_POST['isbn'])) {
    $warnings[] = 'ISBN should be 10 digits';
  }
  // Published should be non-empty
  if(!$_POST['publisher']) {
    $warnings[] = 'Please enter publisher';
  }
  // Year should be 4 digits
  if(!preg_match('~^\d{4}$~', $_POST['year'])) {
    $warnings[] = 'Year should be 4 digits';
  }
  // Sumary should be non-empty
  if(!$_POST['summary']) {
    $warnings[] = 'Please enter summary';
  }
  // If there are no errors, we can update the database
  // If there was book ID passed, update that book
  if(count($warnings) == 0) {
    if(@$book['id']) {
      $sql = "UPDATE books SET title=" . $conn>quote($_POST['title']) .
        ', author=' . $conn->quote($_POST['author']) .
        ', isbn=' . $conn->quote($_POST['isbn']) .
        ', publisher=' . $conn->quote($_POST['publisher']) .
        ', year=' . $conn->quote($_POST['year']) .
        ', summary=' . $conn->quote($_POST['summary']) .
        " WHERE id=$book[id]";
    }
    else {
      $sql = "INSERT INTO books(title, author, isbn, publisher,
              year,summary) VALUES(" .
        $conn->quote($_POST['title']) .
```

```
                  ', ' . $conn->quote($_POST['author']) .
                  ', ' . $conn->quote($_POST['isbn']) .
                  ', ' . $conn->quote($_POST['publisher']) .
                  ', ' . $conn->quote($_POST['year']) .
                  ', ' . $conn->quote($_POST['summary']) .
                  ')';
        }

        // Now we are updating the DB.
        // We wrap this into a try/catch block
        // as an exception can get thrown if
        // the ISBN is already in the table
        try
        {
          $conn->query($sql);
          // If we are here that means that no error
          // We can return back to books listing
          header("Location: books.php");
          exit;
        }
        catch(PDOException $e)
        {
          $warnings[] = 'Duplicate ISBN entered. Please correct';
        }
      }
    }
    else {
      // Form was not submitted.
      // Populate the $_POST array with the book's details
      $_POST = $book;
    }

    // Display the header
    showHeader('Edit Book');
    // If we have any warnings, display them now
    if(count($warnings)) {
      echo "<b>Please correct these errors:</b><br>";
      foreach($warnings as $w)
      {
        echo "- ", htmlspecialchars($w), "<br>";
      }
    }
    // Now display the form
    ?>
    <form action="editBook.php" method="post">
      <table border="1" cellpadding="3">
```

```
<tr>
  <td>Title</td>
  <td>
    <input type="text" name="title"
        value="<?=htmlspecialchars($_POST['title'])?>">
  </td>
</tr>
<tr>
  <td>Author</td>
  <td>
    <select name="author">
      <option value="">Please select...</option>
      <?php foreach($authors as $id=>$author) { ?>
        <option value="<?=$id?>"
          <?= $id == $_POST['author'] ? 'selected' : ''?>>
          <?=htmlspecialchars($author)?>
        </option>
      <?php } ?>
    </select>
  </td>
</tr>
<tr>
  <td>ISBN</td>
  <td>
    <input type="text" name="isbn"
        value="<?=htmlspecialchars($_POST['isbn'])?>">
  </td>
</tr>
<tr>
  <td>Publisher</td>
  <td>
    <input type="text" name="publisher"
        value="<?=htmlspecialchars($_POST['publisher'])?>">
  </td>
</tr>
<tr>
  <td>Year</td>
  <td>
    <input type="text" name="year"
        value="<?=htmlspecialchars($_POST['year'])?>">
  </td>
</tr>
<tr>
  <td>Summary</td>
  <td>
    <textarea name="summary"><?=htmlspecialchars(
                              $_POST['summary'])?></textarea>
```

```
        </td>
      </tr>
      <tr>
        <td colspan="2" align="center">
          <input type="submit" name="submit" value="Save">
        </td>
      </tr>
      </table>
      <?php if(@$book['id']) { ?>
        <input type="hidden" name="book" value="<?=$book['id']?>">
      <?php } ?>
    </form>
    <?php
    // Display footer
    showFooter();
```

The code is rather self-documenting, but let's briefly go through its main parts. Lines 12 to 23 deal with fetching the book details would be edited if the page was requested with the book ID. These details are stored in the $book variable. Note how we explicitly cast the request parameter book to integer so that no SQL injection can occur (line 13). If no book ID is provided, we set it to an empty array. Note how we call the closeCursor() function and then assign the $q variable to null. This is necessary as we are going to reuse the connection object.

Lines 26 to 33 prepare the list of authors. As our system allows exactly one author per book, we will create a select box field listing all the authors.

Line 35 checks whether there was a submission of the form. If the test is successful, the script validates every field (lines 37 to 68). Every failed validation is appended to a list of warnings. (The $warnings variable is initialized with an empty array.) We will use this list to see whether validations were successful and to store error messages if they weren't.

Lines 69 to 94 build the actual SQL for update. The final SQL depends on whether we are updating a book (when the $book array will contain the **id** key), or adding a new one. Note how we quote every column value prior to query execution.

Lines 95 to 112 try to execute the query. It may fail if the user has entered a duplicate ISBN so we wrap the code in a try...catch block. If an exception does get thrown, the catch block will append the corresponding warning to the $warnings array. If everything works without an error, the script redirects to the books listing page where you should see the changes.

Lines 113 to 118 get executed if there was no submission of the form. Here the $_POST array gets populated with the contents of the $books variable. We do this because we will use the $_POST array to display form fields' values later in the code.

Note how we display error messages (if any) on lines 122 to 129 and the select box on lines 141 to 154. (We are looking through all authors and if the author's ID matches this book author's ID then that author is marked as the selected option.) Also, the other form fields are rendered using the htmlspecialchars() function applied to the items of the $_POST array. Lines 189 to 191 will add a hidden field to the form that contains the ID of the currently edited book (if any).

Modern web applications employ client-side validation in addition to server-side validation of user-supplied data. Though this is not in the scope of this book, you might consider browser-based validation in your projects to increase responsiveness and potentially decrease load of your web server.

Now, we should link to the newly created page from the books.php page. We will provide an *Edit this book* link for every listed book as well as an *Add book* link under the table. I will not reproduce the whole books.php source here, just the lines that should be changed. So, lines 32 to 48 should be replaced with the following:

```php
<?php
// Now iterate over every row and display it
while($r = $q->fetch())
{
    ?>
    <tr>
      <td><ahref="author.php?id=<?=$r['authorId']?>">
          <?=htmlspecialchars("$r[firstName] $r[lastName]")?></a></td>
      <td><?=htmlspecialchars($r['title'])?></td>
      <td><?=htmlspecialchars($r['isbn'])?></td>
      <td><?=htmlspecialchars($r['publisher'])?></td>
      <td><?=htmlspecialchars($r['year'])?></td>
      <td><?=htmlspecialchars($r['summary'])?></td>
      <td>
        <a href="editBook.php?book=<?=$r['id']?>">Edit</a>
      </td>
    </tr>
    <?php
}
?>
```

The following should be added just before the call to the showFooter() function so that the four lines look like this:

```php
<a href="editBook.php">Add book...</a>
<?php
// Display footer
showFooter();
```

Now, if you again navigate to the `books.php` page you should see the following window:

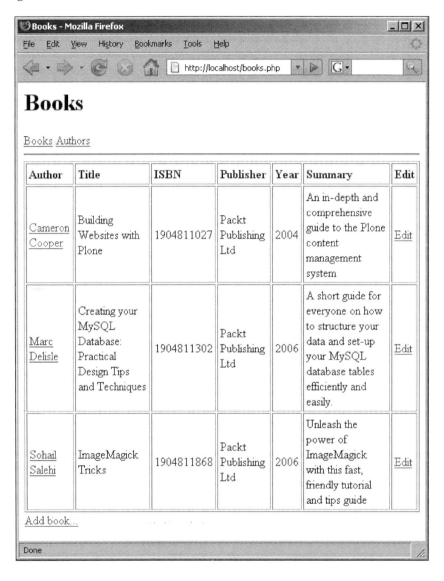

To see how our edit book page looks, click on any **Edit** link in the last column of the table. You should see the following form:

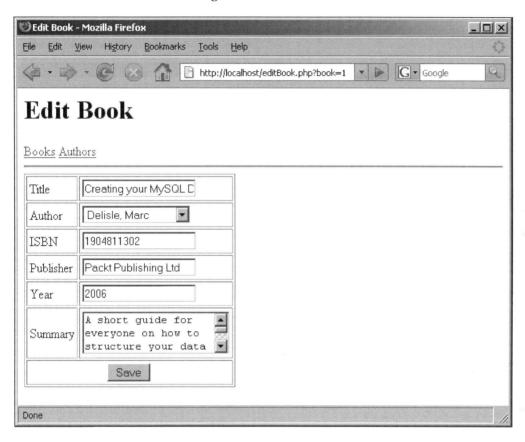

Let's see how our form works. It is validating every form field that gets sent to the database. If there is any validation error, the form will not update the database and prompt the user to correct his submission. For example, try changing the author select box to the default option (labeled *Please select…*) and editing the ISBN to be 5 digits long.

If you click the **Save** button, you should see that the form displays following error messages:

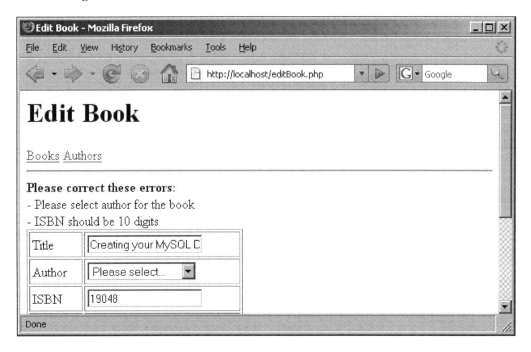

Now correct the errors and try to change the ISBN to 1904811027. This ISBN is already used in our database by another book, so the form will again display an error. You can further test the form by adding a book. You might also want to test how it works with SQLite.

Creating the Edit Author Page

Our application still lacks the add/edit author functionality. This page will be somewhat simpler than the edit book page because it will not have the select box for authors and no unique index. (You may want to create a unique index on the author's first and last name columns to prevent duplicates there too, but we will leave this up to you.)

Let's call this page editAuthor.php. Here is its source code:

```php
<?php

/**
 * This page allows to add or edit an author
 * PDO Library Management example application
```

```
 * @author Dennis Popel
 */
// Don't forget the include
include('common.inc.php');

// See if we have the author ID passed in the request
$id = (int)$_REQUEST['author'];
if($id) {
  // We have the ID, get the author details from the table
  $q = $conn->query("SELECT * FROM authors WHERE id=$id");
  $author = $q->fetch(PDO::FETCH_ASSOC);
  $q->closeCursor();
  $q = null;
}
else {
  // We are creating a new book
  $author = array();
}
// Now see if the form was submitted
if($_POST['submit']) {
  // Validate every field
  $warnings = array();
  // First name should be non-empty
  if(!$_POST['firstName']) {
    $warnings[] = 'Please enter first name';
  }
  // Last name should be non-empty
  if(!$_POST['lastName']) {
    $warnings[] = 'Please enter last name';
  }
  // Bio should be non-empty
  if(!$_POST['bio']) {
    $warnings[] = 'Please enter bio';
  }

  // If there are no errors, we can update the database
  // If there was book ID passed, update that book
  if(count($warnings) == 0) {
    if(@$author['id']) {
      $sql = "UPDATE authors SET firstName=" .
          $co>quote($_POST['firstName']) .
        ', lastName=' . $conn->quote($_POST['lastName']) .
        ', bio=' . $conn->quote($_POST['bio']) .
        " WHERE id=$author[id]";
```

```php
        }
        else {
          $sql = "INSERT INTO authors(firstName, lastName, bio) VALUES(" .
            $conn->quote($_POST['firstName']) .
            ', ' . $conn->quote($_POST['lastName']) .
            ', ' . $conn->quote($_POST['bio']) .
            ')';
        }
        $conn->query($sql);
        header("Location: authors.php");
        exit;
      }
    }
    else {
      // Form was not submitted.
      // Populate the $_POST array with the author's details
      $_POST = $author;
    }

    // Display the header
    showHeader('Edit Author');

    // If we have any warnings, display them now
    if(count($warnings)) {
      echo "<b>Please correct these errors:</b><br>";
      foreach($warnings as $w)
      {
        echo "- ", htmlspecialchars($w), "<br>";
      }
    }

    // Now display the form
    ?>
    <form action="editAuthor.php" method="post">
      <table border="1" cellpadding="3">
      <tr>
        <td>First name</td>
        <td>
          <input type="text" name="firstName"
              value="<?=htmlspecialchars($_POST['firstName'])?>">
        </td>
      </tr>
      <tr>
        <td>Last name</td>
        <td>
          <input type="text" name="lastName"
              value="<?=htmlspecialchars($_POST['lastName'])?>">
```

```
        </td>
      </tr>
      <tr>
        <td>Bio</td>
        <td>
          <textarea name="bio"><?=htmlspecialchars($_POST['bio'])?>
          </textarea>
        </td>
      </tr>
      <tr>
        <td colspan="2" align="center">
            <input type="submit" name="submit" value="Save">
        </td>
      </tr>
      </table>
      <?php if(@$author['id']) { ?>
        <input type="hidden" name="author" value="<?=$author['id']?>">
      <?php } ?>
    </form>
    <?php
    // Display footer
    showFooter();
```

This source is built in the same way as the editBook.php page so you should be able to follow it easily.

We will link to the editAuthors.php page in the same way as we linked to the editBook.php page from the books.php page. Edit the authors.php file and change lines 30-41 to the following:

```
    while($r = $q->fetch(PDO::FETCH_ASSOC))
    {
      ?>
      <tr>
        <td><?=htmlspecialchars($r['firstName'])?></td>
        <td><?=htmlspecialchars($r['lastName'])?></td>
        <td><?=htmlspecialchars($r['bio'])?></td>
        <td>
          <a href="editAuthor.php?author=<?=$r['id']?>">Edit</a>
        </td>
      </tr>
      <?php
    }
```

Add the following line just before the last PHP block:

```
<a href="editAuthor.php">Add Author...</a>
```

Now, if you refresh the `authors.php` page you will see the following:

You can click the **Edit** links in the rightmost column to edit every author's details. You can try submitting the form with empty values to see that invalid submissions will be rejected. Also, you can try and add a new author to the system. After you successfully do this, you may want to go back to books listing and edit some book. You will see that newly created author is available in the **authors** select box.

Securing against Uncaught Exceptions

As we have seen previously, we place the *try...catch* blocks around code that can throw exceptions. However, in very rare cases, there might be some unexpected exceptions. We can imitate such an exception by modifying one of the queries so that it contains some malformed SQL. For example, let's edit `authors.php`, line 16 to the following:

```
$q = $conn->query("SELECT * FROM authors ORDER BY lastName,
                   firstName");
```

Now try to navigate to `authors.php` with your browser to see that an uncaught exception has occurred. To correctly handle this situation, we either should create an exception handler or wrap every block of code that calls `PDO` or `PDOStatement` class methods in a *try...catch* block.

Let's see how we can create the exception handler. This is an easier approach as it does not require changing lots of code. However, for big applications this may be bad practice as handling exceptions, where they occur may be more secure and better recovery logic can be applied.

However, with our simple application we can use the global exception handler. It will just use the `showError()` function to say that the site is under maintenance:

```
/**
 * This is the default exception handler
 * @param Exception $e   the uncaught exception
 */
function exceptionHandler($e)
{
  showError("Sorry, the site is under maintenance\n" .
                  $e->getMessage());
}

// Set the global excpetion handler
set_exception_handler('exceptionHandler');
```

Place this into `common.inc.php`, just before the connection creation code block. If you refresh the `authors.php` page now, you will see that the handler gets called.

It is always a good idea to have the default exception handler. As you have noticed, unhandled exceptions expose too much sensitive information including database connection details. Also, in real world applications the error pages should not display any information about the type of the error. (Note that our example application does.) The default handler should write to the error log and alert site maintainers about the error.

Summary

In this chapter, we examined how PDO handles errors and introduced exceptions. Also, we investigated the sources of errors and saw how to counter them.

Our sample application was extended with some real-world administration functionality that uses data validation and is secured against SQL injection attacks. Of course, they should also allow database modifications only to certain users based on login names and passwords. However, this is beyond the scope of this book.

In the next chapter, we will look at another very important aspect of PDO and database programming in general—using prepared statements. We will see how our administration pages can be simplified with their help, leading to less code and better maintenance.

4

Prepared Statements

In the previous chapters, we have looked at the basics of PDO, and you may have noticed that most of its functionality resembles the traditional extensions used to connect to databases. The only new thing is exceptions, but even that can be similar to traditional error handling.

In this chapter we will look at a new concept that was not present in PHP before PDO: prepared statements. We will see how they can further simplify our code and even lead to better performance. We will also look at how PDO works with BLOBs—all in a database-independent manner, of course.

Regarding our library management application, we will rewrite the edit/update functionality added in the previous chapter so as to facilitate prepared statements, as well as add support for book cover images, which we will keep in the database.

Prepared Statements

A **prepared statement** is a template for executing one or more SQL queries against the database. The idea behind prepared statements is that, with queries that use the same syntax but different values, it is much faster to pre-process the syntax once and then execute it several times using different parameters. Consider the following task. We have to insert the names of several new authors into our database. Of course, we can use command line client or the add author page we recently created, but we decide to use a PHP script.

Let's assume that the authors to be added are kept in a PHP array:

```
$authors = array(
  array(
    'firstName' => 'Alexander',
    'lastName' => 'Dumas',
```

```
        'bio' => 'Alexandre Dumas was a French writer, best known for his
                  numerous historical novels of high adventure which have
                  made him one of the most widely read French authors in
                  the world.'),
    array(
        'firstName' => 'Ivan',
        'lastName' => 'Franko',
        'bio' => 'Ivan Franko was a Ukrainian poet, writer, social and
                  literary critic, and journalist. In addition to his own
                  literary work, he translated the works of William
                  Shakespeare, Lord Byron, Dante, Victor Hugo, Goethe and
                  Schiller into the Ukrainian language.'));
```

This is a two-dimensional array, through which we will iterate using a `foreach` loop so as to insert both the authors' details into the database.

```
foreach($authors as $author)
{
  $conn->query(
    'INSERT INTO authors(firstName, lastName, bio) VALUES(' .
                            $conn->quote($author['firstName']) .
    ',' . $conn->quote($author['lastName']) .
    ',' . $conn->quote($author['bio'])')' .
  );
}
```

As you can see, we create an SQL statement on each iteration for every author and take care of quoting all the parameters.

With prepared statements, we can construct the query just once and execute it any number of times by just passing different values to it. Our code would then look like this:

```
$stmt = $conn->prepare('INSERT INTO authors(firstName, lastName, bio)
                        VALUES(?, ?, ?)');

foreach($authors as $author)
{
  $stmt->execute(
    array($author['firstName'], $author['lastName'],
      $author['bio']));
}
```

From the above code snippet, you can see that a prepared statement is first *prepared* by calling the PDO::prepare() method. This method accepts a string containing an SQL command where the values that change are replaced with question mark characters. The call returns an object of class PDOStatement. Then in the loop we call the statement's execute() method rather than PDO::query() method.

The PDOStatement::execute() method accepts an array of values, which are inserted into the SQL query in place of the question marks. The number and order of elements in that array must be same as the number and match the order of question marks in the query template passed to PDO::prepare().

You must have noticed that we don't use PDO::quote() in the code—PDO takes care of proper quoting of the incoming values.

Positional and Named Placeholders

The previous example used question marks to designate the position of values in the prepared statement. That's why these question marks are called **positional placeholders**. When using them you must take care of proper order of the elements in the array that you are passing to the PDOStatement::execute() method. While they are quick to write, they may become a source for hard-to-track errors, especially when you change the query columns. To protect yourself, against this you can use the so-called **named placeholders**, which consist of descriptive names preceded by a colon, instead of question marks.

With named placeholders, we can rewrite the code to insert the two authors in the following way:

```
$stmt = $conn->prepare(
        'INSERT INTO authors(firstName, lastName, bio) ' .
        'VALUES(:first, :last, :bio)');

foreach($authors as $author)
{
  $stmt->execute(
    array(
      ':first' => $author['firstName'],
      ':last' => $author['lastName'],
      ':bio' => $author['bio'])
  );
}
```

As you can see, we replaced the three question marks with named placeholders and then in the call to PDOStatement::execute() we supplied an array of key-value pairs where keys are the corresponding named placeholders and values are the data that we want to insert into the database.

With named placeholders, the order of the elements in the array is not significant, only the association matters. For example, we could rewrite the loop as follows:

```
foreach($authors as $author)
{
  $stmt->execute(
    array(
      ':bio' => $author['bio'],
      ':last' => $author['lastName'],
      ':first' => $author['firstName'])
  );
}
```

With positional placeholders, however, we can pass the values of the $author array to the PDOStatement::execute() method as long as we are sure that the order of its elements matches the order of the placeholders:

```
$stmt = $conn->prepare(
    'INSERT INTO authors(firstName, lastName, bio) VALUES(?, ?, ?)');
foreach($authors as $author)
{
  $stmt->execute(array_values($author));
}
```

Note how we used the array_values() function to get rid of the string keys and convert the associative array to a list.

If we supply an array of values that do not match the number of placeholders in the query to PDOStatement::execute() or we pass an associative array to a statement that uses positional placeholders (or a list to a statement, which uses named placeholders), this will be treated as an error and an exception will be thrown (provided that exceptions have been enabled previously in a call to PDO::setAttribute() method).

There is one important thing to note about the usage of placeholders. They cannot be used as a part of a value that you pass to the database. This is best demonstrated with an example of invalid usage:

```
$stmt = $conn->prepare("SELECT * FROM authors WHERE lastName
                        LIKE '%?%'");
$stmt->execute(array($_GET['name']));
```

This must be rewritten as follows:

```
$stmt = $conn->prepare("SELECT * FROM authors WHERE lastName
                               LIKE ?");
$stmt->execute(array('%' . $_GET['name'] . '%'));
```

The idea here is, not to put the placeholder inside a string in the SQL template—this has to be done in the call to PDOStatement::execute() method.

Prepared Statements and Bound Values

The examples above used the so-called **unbound statements**. This means that we were supplying the values for the query in an array passed to the PDOStatement:: execute() method. PDO also supports **bound statements** where you can explicitly bind an immediate value or a variable to a named or positional placeholder.

To bind an immediate value to a statement, the PDOStatement::bindValue() method is used. This method accepts the placeholder identifier and a value. The placeholder identifier is the 1-based index of the question mark in the query for positional placeholders or the name of the named placeholder. For example, we could rewrite the example with positional placeholders to use bound values in the following way:

```
$stmt = $conn->prepare(
     'INSERT INTO authors(firstName, lastName, bio) VALUES(?, ?, ?)');
     foreach($authors as $author)
{
  $stmt->bindValue(1, $author['firstName']);
  $stmt->bindValue(2, $author['lastName']);
  $stmt->bindValue(3, $author['bio']);
  $stmt->execute();
}
```

If you prefer named placeholders, you can write:

```
$stmt = $conn->prepare(
        'INSERT INTO authors(firstName, lastName, bio) ' .
        'VALUES(:last, :first, :bio)');
   foreach($authors as $author)
{
  $stmt->bindValue(':first', $author['firstName']);
  $stmt->bindValue(':last', $author['lastName']);
  $stmt->bindValue(':bio', $author['bio']);
  $stmt->execute();
}
```

As you can see, in both cases we don't supply anything in the call to
PDOStatement::execute(). Again, as with unbound statements, if you don't bind a
value for every placeholder, the call to PDOStatement::execute() will fail, leading
to an exception.

PDO can also bind result set columns to PHP variables for SELECT queries. These
variables will be modified with corresponding column values on every call to
PDOStatement::fetch(). This is an alternative to fetching the result set row as an
array or an object as discussed in Chapter 2. Consider the following example:

```
$stmt = $conn->prepare('SELECT firstName, lastName FROM authors');
$stmt->execute();
$stmt->bindColumn(1, $first);
$stmt->bindColumn(2, $last);
while($stmt->fetch(PDO::FETCH_BOUND))
{
   echo "$last, $first <br>";
}
```

This will render all the authors in the table. The variables are bound in the call to the
PDOStatement::bindColumn() method, which expects the first parameter to be the
1-based index of the column in the result set or the column name as returned from
the database, and the second parameter is the variable to be updated.

Note that when using bound columns, the PDOStatement::fetch() method
should be called with the PDO::FETCH_BOUND mode, or this should be preset
with a PDOStatement::setFetchMode(PDO::FETCH_BOUND) call. Also, the call
to the PDOStatement::bindColumn() method must be made after the call to
PDOStatement::execute() method so that PDO knows how many columns there
are in the result set.

Let's get back to our library application now and enhance it with some prepared
statements. Since the only pages that rely on the values supplied by the user are
add/edit a book and *add/edit an author*, we will rewrite the two corresponding scripts,
editBook.php and editAuthor.php.

Of course, we will only rewrite those bits of the code that update the database.
For editBook.php these are lines 65 to 102. I will present these lines here for
your convenience:

```
if(@$book['id']) {
   $sql = "UPDATE books SET title=" . $conn->quote($_POST['title']) .
           ', author=' . $conn->quote($_POST['author']) .
           ', isbn=' . $conn->quote($_POST['isbn']) .
           ', publisher=' . $conn->quote($_POST['publisher']) .
```

```
        ', year=' . $conn->quote($_POST['year']) .
        ', summary=' . $conn->quote($_POST['summary']) .
        " WHERE id=$book[id]";
    }
    else {
      $sql = "INSERT INTO books(title, author, isbn, publisher, year,
              summary) VALUES(" . $conn->quote($_POST['title']) .
        ', ' . $conn->quote($_POST['author']) .
        ', ' . $conn->quote($_POST['isbn']) .
        ', ' . $conn->quote($_POST['publisher']) .
        ', ' . $conn->quote($_POST['year']) .
        ', ' . $conn->quote($_POST['summary']) .
        ')';
    }


    // Now we are updating the DB.
    // We wrap this into a try/catch block
    // as an exception can get thrown if
    // the ISBN is already in the table.
    try
    {
      $conn->query($sql);
      // If we are here, then there is no error.
      // We can return back to books listing
      header("Location: books.php");
      exit;
    }
    catch(PDOException $e)
    {
      $warnings[] = 'Duplicate ISBN entered. Please correct';
    }
```

As we can see, the part that constructs the query is very long. With a prepared statement, this code snippet can be rewritten as follows:

```
    if(@$book['id']) {
      $sql = "UPDATE books SET title=?, author=?, isbn=?, publisher=?
                  year=?, summary=? WHERE id=$book[id]";
    }
    else {
      $sql = "INSERT INTO books(title, author, isbn, publisher, year,
                  summary) VALUES(?, ?, ?, ?, ?, ?)";
```

```
}
$stmt = $conn->prepare($sql);

// Now we are updating the DB.
// We wrap this into a try/catch block
// as an exception can get thrown if
// the ISBN is already in the table.
try
{
  $stmt->execute(array($_POST['title'], $_POST['author'],
    $_POST['isbn'], $_POST['publisher'], $_POST['year'],
    $_POST['summary']));
  // If we are here, then there is no error.
  // We can return back to books listing.
  header("Location: books.php");
  exit;
}
catch(PDOException $e)
{
  $warnings[] = 'Duplicate ISBN entered. Please correct';
}
```

We follow the same logic—if we are editing an existing book, we construct an UPDATE query. If we are adding a new book, then we have to use an INSERT query. The $sql variable will hold the appropriate statement template. In both cases, the statement has six positional placeholders, and I intentionally hard-coded the book ID into the UPDATE query so that we can create and execute the statement regardless of the required operation.

After we have instantiated the statement, we wrap the call to its execute() method into a *try...catch* block as an exception that may get thrown if the ISBN already existed in the database. Upon successful execution of the statement we redirect the browser to the books listing page. If the call fails, we alert the user with a note that the ISBN is incorrect (or that the book already exists in the database).

You can see that our code is now much shorter. Also, we don't need to quote the values as the prepared statement does this for us. Now you can play with this a bit and change the databases between MySQL and SQLite in common.inc.php to see that prepared statements work for both of them. You may also want to rewrite this code to use named placeholders instead of positional ones. If you do, remember to supply placeholder names in the array passed to the PDOStatement::execute() method.

Now let's look at the corresponding code block in `editAuthor.php` (lines 42 to 59):

```
if(@$author['id']) {
  $sql = "UPDATE authors SET firstName=" .
          $conn->quote($_POST['firstName']) .
          ', lastName=' . $conn->quote($_POST['lastName']) .
          ', bio=' . $conn->quote($_POST['bio']) .
          " WHERE id=$author[id]";
}
else {
  $sql = "INSERT INTO authors(firstName, lastName, bio) VALUES(" .
          $conn->quote($_POST['firstName']) .
    ', ' . $conn->quote($_POST['lastName']) .
    ', ' . $conn->quote($_POST['bio']) .
    ')';
}

$conn->query($sql);
header("Location: authors.php");
exit;
```

As we don't expect an exception here, the code is shorter. Now let's rewrite it to use a prepared statement:

```
if(@$author['id']) {
  $sql = "UPDATE authors SET firstName=?, lastName=?, bio=?
              WHERE id=$author[id]";
}
else {
  $sql = "INSERT INTO authors(firstName, lastName, bio)
              VALUES(?, ?, ?)";
}
$stmt = $conn->prepare($sql);
$stmt->execute(array($_POST['firstName'], $_POST['lastName'],
                  $_POST['bio']));
header("Location: authors.php");
exit;
```

Again, depending on the required operation, we create the SQL template and assign it to the `$sql` variable. Then we instantiate the PDOStatement object and call its `execute` method with the author's details. As our query should never fail (except for an unforeseen database failure) we don't expect an exception here and redirect to the authors listing pages.

Make sure that you test this code with both MySQL and SQLite.

Working with BLOBs

Let's now extend our application so that we can upload the books' cover images and display them. Just as with traditional database access, we will use a **BLOB field** in the books table for this purpose, as well as a **varchar field** to store the image's MIME type, which we will need to supply to the browser along with the image data. Also, we will need another script that will fetch the image data from the table and pass it to the browser. (We will reference this script from the `<img>` tag.).

Traditionally, we would not care that we are inserting a BLOB column into the calls to `mysql_query()` or `sqlite_query()` — we would just make sure that they are properly quoted. With PDO, however, things are different. PDO works with BLOB columns with the help of streams and prepared statements.

Let's look at the following example:

```
$blob = fopen('/path/to/file.jpg', 'rb');
$stmt = $conn->prepare("INSERT INTO images(data) VALUES(?)");
$stmt->bindParam(1, $blob, PDO::PARAM_LOB);
$stmt->execute();
```

As you can see, we open the file to be inserted with the `fopen()` function for reading in the binary mode (so that we don't have problems with newline characters across platforms) and then bind the file handle to the statement in the call to the `PDOStatement::bindParam()` method specifying the `PDO::PARAM_LOB` flag (so that PDO understands that we have bound a file handle rather than an immediate value).

In the call to the `PDOStatement::execute()` method, PDO will read the data from the file and pass it to the database.

> If you are wondering why PDO works in such a way, a short explanation is that, if your BLOB is very large, the query may fail. Normally database servers have a setting that limits communication packet size. (You can compare this with `post_max_size` PHP setting). If you are passing relatively large string inside an SQL `INSERT` or `UPDATE` statement, it may exceed that packet size and the query will fail. With streams, PDO ensures that data is sent in smaller packets so that the query executes successfully.

The BLOBs should also be read with streams. So to retrieve a BLOB column inserted in the above example, the following code could be used:

```
$id = (int)$_GET['id'];
$stmt = $db->prepare("SELECT data FROM images WHERE id=$id");
$stmt->execute();
```

```
$stmt->bindColumn(1, $blob, PDO::PARAM_LOB);
$stmt->fetch(PDO::FETCH_BOUND);
$data = stream_get_contents($blob);
```

In this case, the `$blob` variable will be a stream resource that can be read with stream-handling functions. Here we used the `stream_get_contents()` function to read all the data into the `$data` variable. If we want to directly return the data to the browser (as we will in our application), we could employ the `fpassthru()` function.

As of this writing (PHP version 5.2.3), the returned blob column is not a stream but the actual data contained in the column (string). Please refer to PHP bug #40913 at `http://bugs.php.net/bug.php?id=40913` for details. Hence the last line in the above code snippet is not required, the `$blob` variable will hold the actual data. The source of showCover.php file below treats the returned data as a string rather than a blob, so that the code works in current PHP version.

So, let's begin with altering our database and adding the new columns to it:

```
mysql> alter table books add column coverMime varchar(20);
Query OK, 3 rows affected (0.02 sec)
Records: 3  Duplicates: 0  Warnings: 0

mysql> alter table books add column coverImage blob(24000);
Query OK, 3 rows affected (0.02 sec)
Records: 3  Duplicates: 0  Warnings: 0
```

You can also execute these queries in the SQLite command line client without modifications. Now, let's modify the `editBook.php` file. We will add another field to the existing form. This line will allow the user to upload the cover image and enhance the form validation to check whether the user has really uploaded an image (by examining the MIME type of the uploaded file).

We will also allow the user to modify the book's details without resubmitting the cover image file. To achieve this, we will update the cover columns only when there has been a successful file upload. So our script logic will use two queries. The first one will update or create the book record, and the second will update the `coverMime` and `coverImage` columns.

With this in mind, the `editBook.php` file will look like the following:

```php
<?php

/**
 * This page allows adding or editing a book
 * PDO Library Management example application
 * @author Dennis Popel
 */
```

```
// Don't forget the include
include('common.inc.php');

// See if we have the book ID passed in the request
$id = (int)$_REQUEST['book'];
if($id) {
  // we have the ID, get the book details from the table
  $q = $conn->query("SELECT * FROM books WHERE id=$id");
  $book = $q->fetch(PDO::FETCH_ASSOC);
  $q->closeCursor();
  $q = null;
}
else {
  // we are creating a new book
  $book = array();
}

// Now get the list of all authors' first and last names
// we will need it to create the dropdown box for author
$authors = array();
$q = $conn->query("SELECT id, lastName, firstName FROM authors ORDER
                   BY lastName, firstName");
$q->setFetchMode(PDO::FETCH_ASSOC);
while($a = $q->fetch())
{
  $authors[$a['id']] = "$a[lastName], $a[firstName]";
}

// Now see if the form was submitted
if($_POST['submit']) {
  // Validate every field
  $warnings = array();
  // Title should be non-empty
  if(!$_POST['title']) {
    $warnings[] = 'Please enter book title';
  }
  // Author should be a key in the $authors array
  if(!array_key_exists($_POST['author'], $authors)) {
    $warnings[] = 'Please select author for the book';
  }
  // ISBN should be a 10-digit number
  if(!preg_match('~^\d{10}$~', $_POST['isbn'])) {
    $warnings[] = 'ISBN should be 10 digits';
  }
  // Published should be non-empty
  if(!$_POST['publisher']) {
```

```
  $warnings[] = 'Please enter publisher';
}
// Year should be 4 digits
if(!preg_match('~^\d{4}$~', $_POST['year'])) {
  $warnings[] = 'Year should be 4 digits';
}
// Summary should be non-empty
if(!$_POST['summary']) {
  $warnings[] = 'Please enter summary';
}

// Now validate the file upload
$uploadSuccess = false;
if(is_uploaded_file($_FILES['cover']['tmp_name'])) {
  // See if the file is an image
  if(!preg_match('~image/.+~', $_FILES['cover']['type'])
    || filesize($_FILES['cover']['tmp_name']) > 24000) {
    $warnings[] = 'Please upload an image file less than 24K
                  in size';
  }
  else {
    // Set a flag that upload is successful
    $uploadSuccess = true;
  }
}

// If there are no errors, we can update the database
// If there was book ID passed, update that book
if(count($warnings) == 0) {
  if(@$book['id']) {
    $sql = "UPDATE books SET title=?, author=?, isbn=?,
              publisher=?, year=?, summary=? WHERE
                    id=$book[id]";
  }
  else {
    $sql = "INSERT INTO books(title, author, isbn, publisher,
              year, summary) VALUES(?, ?, ?, ?, ?, ?)";
  }
  $stmt = $conn->prepare($sql);

  // Now we are updating the DB.
  // we wrap this into a try/catch block
  // as an exception can get thrown if
  // the ISBN is already in the table
  try
```

```php
    {
      $stmt->execute(array($_POST['title'], $_POST['author'],
              $_POST['isbn'], $_POST['publisher'], $_POST['year'],
              $_POST['summary']));
      // If we are here that means that no error
      // Now we can update the cover columns
      // But first we have to get the ID of the newly inserted book
      if(!@$book['id']) {
        $book['id'] = $conn->lastInsertId();
      }
      // Now see if there was an successful upload and
      // update cover image
      if($uploadSuccess) {
        $stmt = $conn->prepare("UPDATE books SET coverMime=?,
                              coverImage=? WHERE id=$book[id]");
        $cover = fopen($_FILES['cover']['tmp_name'], 'rb');
        $stmt->bindValue(1, $_FILES['cover']['type']);
        $stmt->bindParam(2, $cover, PDO::PARAM_LOB);
        $stmt->execute();
      }
      // We can return back to books listing
      header("Location: books.php");
      exit;
    }
    catch(PDOException $e)
    {
      $warnings[] = 'Duplicate ISBN entered. Please correct';
    }
  }
}
else {
  // Form was not submitted.
  // populate the $_POST array with the book's details
  $_POST = $book;
}
// Display the header
showHeader('Edit Book');
// If we have any warnings, display them now
if(count($warnings)) {
  echo "<b>Please correct these errors:</b><br>";
  foreach($warnings as $w)
  {
    echo "- ", htmlspecialchars($w), "<br>";
```

```
    }
}
// Now display the form
?>
<form action="editBook.php" method="post"
    enctype="multipart/form-data">
  <table border="1" cellpadding="3">
  <tr>
    <td>Title</td>
    <td>
      <input type="text" name="title"
        value="<?=htmlspecialchars($_POST['title'])?>">
    </td>
  </tr>
  <tr>
    <td>Author</td>
    <td>
      <select name="author">
        <option value="">Please select...</option>
        <?php foreach($authors as $id=>$author)
        { ?>
          <option value="<?=$id?>"
            <?= $id == $_POST['author'] ? 'selected' : ''?>>
            <?=htmlspecialchars($author)?>
          </option>
        <?php } ?>
      </select>
    </td>
  </tr>
  <tr>
    <td>ISBN</td>
    <td>
      <input type="text" name="isbn"
        value="<?=htmlspecialchars($_POST['isbn'])?>">
    </td>
  </tr>
  <tr>
    <td>Publisher</td>
    <td>
      <input type="text" name="publisher"
        value="<?=htmlspecialchars($_POST['publisher'])?>">
    </td>
  </tr>
  <tr>
```

```
        <td>Year</td>
        <td>
          <input type="text" name="year"
             value="<?=htmlspecialchars($_POST['year'])?>">
        </td>
      </tr>
      <tr>
        <td>Summary</td>
        <td>
         <textareaname="summary"><?=htmlspecialchars($_POST['summary'])?>
         </textarea>
        </td>
      </tr>
      <tr>
        <td>Cover Image</td>

        <td><input type="file" name="cover"></td>
      </tr>
       <?php if(@$book['coverMime'])
      { ?>
        <tr>
          <td>Current Cover</td>
          <td><img src="showCover.php?book=<?=$book['id']?>"></td>
        </tr>
      <? } ?>
       <tr>
        <td colspan="2" align="center">
          <input type="submit" name="submit" value="Save">
        </td>
      </tr>
      </table>
       <?php if(@$book['id']) { ?>
        <input type="hidden" name="book" value="<?=$book['id']?>">
      <?php } ?>
  </form>
   <?php
  // Display footer
  showFooter();
```

The highlighted parts are the bits that we have added or changed. Now, we need to validate our form and the uploaded file (on lines 60 to 73). If there is a successful upload, the $uploadSuccess boolean variable will be set to true, and we will use this value later to see whether we need to update the cover columns. Since we allow the upload to happen for new books too, we use the PDO::lastInsertId() method value (on line 100) to get the ID of the newly created books (otherwise we just use the $books['id'] value). If the upload fails, we add a corresponding warning to the $warnings array and let the existing error logic do its job.

The actual cover image update happens on lines 105 to 110, using the prepared statement and the stream. On our form, see how we add the multipart/form-data attribute to the form tag on line 140. It is needed for the file uploads to work. Also, the form now has a new input field (lines #182-185) allowing us to select and upload a file. The next lines will display the current cover image (if any). Note that the <img> tag references a new file, showCover.php, which we will have to create now:

```php
<?php
/**
 * This script will render a book's cover image
 * PDO Library Management example application
 * @author Dennis Popel
 */
// Don't forget the include
include('common.inc.php');
// See if we have the book ID passed in the request
$id = (int)$_REQUEST['book'];
$stmt = $conn->prepare("SELECT coverMime, coverImage FROM books
                        WHERE id=$id");
$stmt->execute();
$stmt->bindColumn(1, $mime);
$stmt->bindColumn(2, $image, PDO::PARAM_LOB);
$stmt->fetch(PDO::FETCH_BOUND);
header("Content-Type: $mime");
echo $image;
```

Now for a new book, the form looks like this:

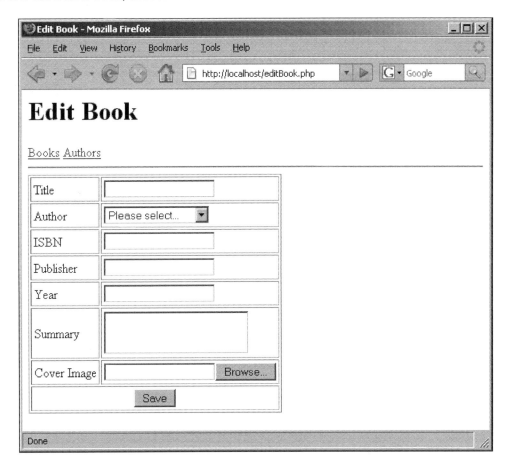

As you can see, there is a new field allowing us to upload the cover image. Since a newly created book does not have any cover image, there is no current cover image. For a book with a cover image the page will look like the following:

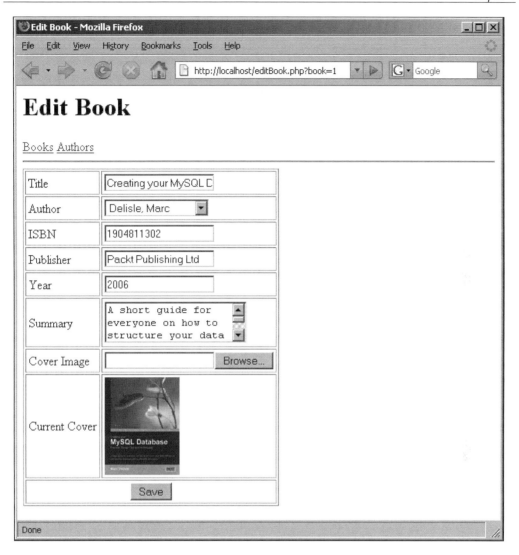

You can now play with the application to see how the form works without uploading the image. (It should preserve the old image if any.) You can also see how it processes files that are too large or non-image files. (It should display a warning above the form.) Make sure that you switch between databases so that we are database-independent.

As the final touch to the cover images, we can reformat the books listing page, books.php, so that the cover images are displayed there too. I will present the new code here with the changed part highlighted:

```php
<?php
/**
 * This page lists all the books we have
 * PDO Library Management example application
 * @author Dennis Popel
 */

// Don't forget the include
include('common.inc.php');

// Display the header
showHeader('Books');

// Issue the query
$q = $conn->query("SELECT authors.id AS authorId, firstName,
                   lastName, books.* FROM authors, books WHERE
                       author=authors.id ORDER BY title");
$q->setFetchMode(PDO::FETCH_ASSOC);

// now create the table
?>
<table width="100%" border="1" cellpadding="3">
<tr style="font-weight: bold">
  <td>Cover</td>
  <td>Author and Title</td>
  <td>ISBN</td>
  <td>Publisher</td>
  <td>Year</td>
  <td>Summary</td>
  <td>Edit</td>
</tr>

<?php
// Now iterate over every row and display it
while($r = $q->fetch())
{
  ?>
  <tr>
    <td>
      <?php if($r['coverMime']) { ?>
        <img src="showCover.php?book=<?=$r['id']?>">
      <?php }
```

```php
      else
      { ?>
        n/a
      <? } ?>
    </td>
    <td>
      <a href="author.php?id=<?=$r['authorId']?>">
        <?=htmlspecialchars("$r[firstName] $r[lastName]")?></a><br/>
      <b><?=htmlspecialchars($r['title'])?></b>
    </td>
    <td><?=htmlspecialchars($r['isbn'])?></td>
    <td><?=htmlspecialchars($r['publisher'])?></td>
    <td><?=htmlspecialchars($r['year'])?></td>
    <td><?=htmlspecialchars($r['summary'])?></td>
    <td>
      <a href="editBook.php?book=<?=$r['id']?>">Edit</a>
    </td>
  </tr>
  <?php
}
?>
</table>

<a href="editBook.php">Add book...</a>
<?php
// Display footer
showFooter();
```

The first cell will contain the image (if any). The author and title are now rendered in the same cell to save table width. Now the Books listing should look something like this:

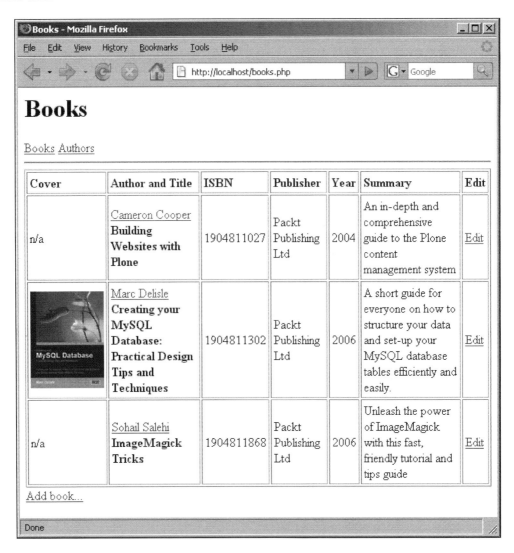

Summary

This chapter introduced us to a new concept: Prepared Statements. We have seen how they simplify our queries and further protect us from SQL syntax errors and code vulnerabilities. We also took a look at how to work with BLOBs using streams so that we don't run the risk of query failures. Our application can now be used to upload and show cover images for the books in the database.

In the next chapter, we shall see how to determine the number of rows in a result set, which is necessary to paginate long lists of items. (The most common example is a search engine that breaks the result list into 10 results per page.) Also, we will familiarize ourselves with a new concept: scrollable cursors that will allow us to fetch a subset of rows from a result set starting at a specified position.

5

Handling Rowsets

Real life dynamic, data-driven web applications are very different from each other, as their complexity is dictated by the purposes that they serve. However, almost all of them have some common characteristics. One of these characteristics is the ability to paginate long result lists for ease of use and faster page loading times.

Correct pagination requires the calculation of the number of total rows returned from the database, the page size (which is a configurable option), and the number of current page. Based on this data, it is easy to calculate the starting offset into the result set to display only a subset of rows.

In this chapter, we will examine:

- How to retrieve the number of rows in the result sets returned by PDO
- How to fetch results starting at a specified row number

Retrieving the Number of Rows in a Result Set

As we have already discussed in Chapter 2, the `PDOStatement::rowCount()` method does not return the correct number of rows in a query. (It returns zero for both MySQL and SQLite.) The reason for such behavior is that the database management systems do not actually know this number until the last row of the query has been returned. The reason for the `mysql_num_rows()` function (and similar functions for other databases) returns the row count is that it preloads the whole result set into memory when you issue the query.

While it may seem convenient, this behavior is not recommended. If the query returns 20 rows, then the script can afford the memory usage. But what if the query returns several hundred thousands rows? They will all be kept in memory so that, on high traffic sites, the server may run out of resources.

The only logical measure (and the only option available with PDO) is to instruct the database to count the number of rows itself. No matter how complicated the query is, it can be rewritten to use the SQL COUNT() function to return just the number of rows that will satisfy the main query.

Let's take a look at the queries used in our application. (We will only examine the queries that return multiple rows.)

- In books.php we have a query that joins two tables to present the list of books along with their authors :

  ```
  SELECT authors.id AS authorId, firstName, lastName, books.*
  FROM authors, books WHERE author=authors.id ORDER BY title;
  ```

  To get the number of rows that this query returns we should rewrite it to look like the following:

  ```
  SELECT COUNT(*) FROM authors, books WHERE author=authors.id;
  ```

  Note that we don't need the ORDER BY clause here as the order does not really matter for the count of rows.

- In authors.php we simply select all the authors ordered by their last name and then their first name:

  ```
  SELECT * FROM authors ORDER BY lastName, firstName;
  ```

  This simply rewrites to the following:

  ```
  SELECT COUNT(*) FROM authors;
  ```

- Another query that returns multiple rows is in author.php—it retrieves all the books written by a particular author:

  ```
  SELECT * FROM books WHERE author=$id ORDER BY title;
  ```

  This translates to the following:

  ```
  SELECT COUNT(*) FROM books WHERE author=$id;
  ```

As you can see, we rewrote all these queries in a similar way—by replacing the list of columns with COUNT(*) and trimming the ORDER BY clause. With this in mind, we can create a function that will accept a string containing the SQL to be executed and return the number of rows that the query will return. This function will have to perform these simple transformations:

- Replace everything between SELECT and FROM with COUNT(*) in the passed string.
- Remove ORDER BY and all the text after it.

The best way to achieve this transformation is to use regular expressions. As in previous chapters, we will use the PCRE extension. We will put the function into `common.inc.php` as we will call it from various places:

```
/**
 * This function will return the number of rows a query will return
 * @param   string $sql   the SQL query
 * @return  int   the number of rows the query specified will return
 * @throws   PDOException   if the query cannot be executed
 */
function getRowCount($sql)
{
    global $conn;

    $sql = trim($sql);
    $sql = preg_replace('~^SELECT\s.*\sFROM~s', 'SELECT COUNT(*) FROM',
                        $sql);
    $sql = preg_replace('~ORDER\s+BY.*?$~sD', '', $sql);
    $stmt = $conn->query($sql);
    $r = $stmt->fetchColumn(0);
    $stmt->closeCursor();
    return $r;
}
```

Let's run over the function to see what it does:

1. It imports the PDO connection object (`$conn`) into the local function scope.

2. It trims the possible spaces from the beginning and the end of the SQL query.

3. Two calls to `preg_replace()` do the main task of transforming the query.

Note how we use the pattern modifiers—the *s* modifier instructs PCRE to match newline characters with the dot, and the *D* modifier forces the $ to match the end of the whole string (not just before the first newline). We use these modifiers to make sure that the function will work properly with multiline queries.

We will now modify the three scripts to display the number of rows in each table that they return. Let's start with `books.php`:

```
<?php

/**
 * This page lists all the books we have
 * PDO Library Management example application
```

```
 * @author Dennis Popel
 */

// Don't forget the include
include('common.inc.php');

// Display the header
showHeader('Books');

// Get the count of books and issue the query
$sql = "SELECT authors.id AS authorId, firstName, lastName, books.*
        FROM authors, books WHERE author=authors.id ORDER BY title";
$totalBooks = getRowCount($sql);
$q = $conn->query($sql);
$q->setFetchMode(PDO::FETCH_ASSOC);

// now create the table
?>
Total books: <?=$totalBooks?>
<table width="100%" border="1" cellpadding="3">
<tr style="font-weight: bold">
  <td>Cover</td>
  <td>Author and Title</td>
  <td>ISBN</td>
  <td>Publisher</td>
  <td>Year</td>
  <td>Summary</td>
  <td>Edit</td>
</tr>

<?php
// Now iterate over every row and display it
while($r = $q->fetch())
{
  ?>
  <tr>
    <td>
      <?php if($r['coverMime']) { ?>
        <img src="showCover.php?book=<?=$r['id']?>">
      <?php } else { ?>
        n/a
      <? } ?>
    </td>
    <td>
      <a href="author.php?id=<?=$r['authorId']?>"><?=htmlspecialchars
            ("$r[firstName] $r[lastName]")?></a><br/>
      <b><?=htmlspecialchars($r['title'])?></b>
```

```
    </td>
    <td><?=htmlspecialchars($r['isbn'])?></td>
    <td><?=htmlspecialchars($r['publisher'])?></td>
    <td><?=htmlspecialchars($r['year'])?></td>
    <td><?=htmlspecialchars($r['summary'])?></td>
    <td>
      <a href="editBook.php?book=<?=$r['id']?>">Edit</a>
    </td>
  </tr>
  <?php
}
?>
</table>
<a href="editBook.php">Add book...</a>
<?php
// Display footer
showFooter();
```

As you can see, the modifications are pretty straightforward—we use the $sql
variable to hold the query and pass it to both the getRowCount() function and the
$conn->query() method. We also display a message above the table, which tells us
how many books there are in the database.

Now if you refresh the books.php page, you will see the following:

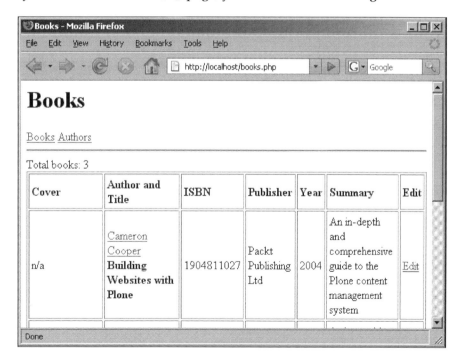

The changes to authors.php are similar:

```php
<?php
/**
 * This page lists all the authors we have
 * PDO Library Management example application
 * @author Dennis Popel
 */

// Don't forget the include
include('common.inc.php');

// Display the header
showHeader('Authors');

// Get the number of authors and issue the query
$sql = "SELECT * FROM authors ORDER BY lastName, firstName";
$totalAuthors = getRowCount($sql);
$q = $conn->query($sql);

// now create the table
?>
Total authors: <?=$totalAuthors?>
<table width="100%" border="1" cellpadding="3">
<tr style="font-weight: bold">
  <td>First Name</td>
  <td>Last Name</td>
  <td>Bio</td>
  <td>Edit</td>
</tr>

<?php
// Now iterate over every row and display it
while($r = $q->fetch(PDO::FETCH_ASSOC))
{
  ?>
  <tr>
    <td><?=htmlspecialchars($r['firstName'])?></td>
    <td><?=htmlspecialchars($r['lastName'])?></td>
    <td><?=htmlspecialchars($r['bio'])?></td>
    <td>
      <a href="editAuthor.php?author=<?=$r['id']?>">Edit</a>
    </td>
  </tr>
  <?php
}
?>
```

```
</table>
<a href="editAuthor.php">Add Author...</a>
<?php
// Display footer
showFooter();
```

The `authors.php` now should display the following:

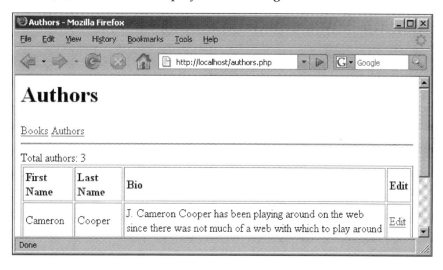

Finally, `author.php` will look like this:

```php
<?php
/**
 * This page shows an author's profile
 * PDO Library Management example application
 * @author Dennis Popel
 */

// Don't forget the include
include('common.inc.php');

// Get the author
$id = (int)$_REQUEST['id'];
$q = $conn->query("SELECT * FROM authors WHERE id=$id");
$author = $q->fetch(PDO::FETCH_ASSOC);
$q->closeCursor();
$q = null;

// Now see if the author is valid - if it's not,
// we have an invalid ID
if(!$author) {
```

```php
  showHeader('Error');
  echo "Invalid Author ID supplied";
  showFooter();
  exit;
}

// Display the header - we have no error
showHeader("Author: $author[firstName] $author[lastName]");

// Now get the number and fetch all the books
$sql = "SELECT * FROM books WHERE author=$id ORDER BY title";
$totalBooks = getRowCount($sql);
$q = $conn->query($sql);
$q->setFetchMode(PDO::FETCH_ASSOC);

// now display everything
?>
<h2>Author</h2>
<table width="60%" border="1" cellpadding="3">
<tr>
  <td><b>First Name</b></td>
  <td><?=htmlspecialchars($author['firstName'])?></td>
</tr>
<tr>
  <td><b>Last Name</b></td>
  <td><?=htmlspecialchars($author['lastName'])?></td>
</tr>
<tr>
  <td><b>Bio</b></td>
  <td><?=htmlspecialchars($author['bio'])?></td>
</tr>
<tr>
  <td><b>Total books</td>
  <td><?=$totalBooks?></td>
</tr>
</table>
<a href="editAuthor.php?author=<?=$author['id']?>">Edit author...</a>

<h2>Books</h2>
<table width="100%" border="1" cellpadding="3">
<tr style="font-weight: bold">
  <td>Title</td>
  <td>ISBN</td>
  <td>Publisher</td>
  <td>Year</td>
  <td>Summary</td>
```

```php
</tr>
<?php
// Now iterate over every book and display it
while($r = $q->fetch()) {
  ?>
  <tr>
    <td><?=htmlspecialchars($r['title'])?></td>
    <td><?=htmlspecialchars($r['isbn'])?></td>
    <td><?=htmlspecialchars($r['publisher'])?></td>
    <td><?=htmlspecialchars($r['year'])?></td>
    <td><?=htmlspecialchars($r['summary'])?></td>
  </tr>
  <?php
}
?>
</table>

<?php
// Display footer
showFooter();
```

The output should look like this. (I scrolled the page down a bit to save space):

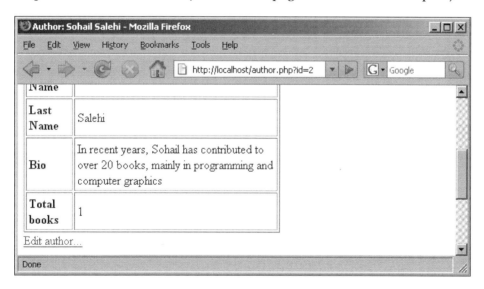

You should switch between MySQL and SQLite in `common.inc.php` to make sure both databases work.

This approach may work for many cases, but is not suitable for all queries. One such example is a query that uses a GROUP BY clause. If you rewrite such query with the getRowCount() function you will get incorrect results as the grouping will be applied and the query will return several rows. (The number of rows will be equal to the number of distinct values in the column you are grouping by.)

Limiting the Number of Rows Returned

Now, when we know how to count the rows in the results set, let's see how we can fetch first N rows only. Here we have two options:

- We can use database-specific features in the SQL query itself.
- We can process the result set ourselves and stop after the required number of rows has been fetched.

Using Database-Specific SQL

If you have been working mainly with MySQL, then you will be familiar with the LIMIT x,y clause. For example, if we want to fetch the first five authors sorted by last name, the following query could be issued:

```
SELECT * FROM authors ORDER BY lastName LIMIT 0, 5;
```

The same thing could be done with the following query:

```
SELECT * FROM authors ORDER BY lastName LIMIT 5 OFFSET 0;
```

The first query will work for MySQL and SQLite, while the second will work for PostgreSQL as well. However, databases like Oracle or MS SQL Server don't use such syntax, so these queries will fail for them.

Processing the Top N Rows Only

As you can see, database-specific SQL does not allow us to solve the task of performing pagination in the database-independent way. However, we can issue the query as we would for all the rows, without the LIMIT....OFFSET clause. After each row has been fetched, we can increase the counter variable, so that we break the loop when we have processed the required amount of rows. The following code snippet could serve this purpose:

```
$q = $conn->query("SELECT * FROM authors ORDER BY lastName,
                    firstName");
$q->setFetchMode(PDO::FETCH_ASSOC);
```

```
$count = 1;
while(($r = $q->fetch()) && $count <= 5)
{
  echo $r['lastName'], '<br>';
  $count++;
}
$q->closeCursor();
$q = null;
```

Note the loop condition—it checks whether the counter variable is less than or equal to 5. (Of course, you can put any number there), as well as it verifies that there still are rows to fetch, as it is important that we break the loop if there are no more rows. (For example, if the table has only 3 rows and we want to show 5 of them we should break after the last row, not after the counter reaches 5.) Note that using database-specific SQL would take care of such a situation for us.

Another important thing is the call to PDOStatement::closeCursor() (as on the second last line in the previous code snippet). It is necessary to tell the database that we don't want more rows. If we don't do this, the subsequent queries issued on the same PDO object will cause exceptions, because database management systems cannot process a new query while they are still sending the rows from the previous query. This is why we had to call this method in author.php.

At present (for PHP version 5.2.1), it may be necessary to unset the statement object by assigning it to null (as in author.php, line 17). On the other hand, at least one CVS snapshot released around April 1, 2007 didn't require closing the cursor at all. However, it is still good practice to call PDOStatement::closeCursor() after you have finished with the cursor.

Starting at an Arbitrary Offset

Now that we know how to process a specified number of rows, we can use the same technique to skip a certain number of rows. Suppose that we want to show authors from 6th to 10th (as though we are showing page 2 when the page size allows for 5 authors per page):

```
$q = $conn->query("SELECT * FROM authors ORDER BY lastName,
                        firstName");
$q->setFetchMode(PDO::FETCH_ASSOC);
$count = 1;
while(($r = $q->fetch()) && $count <= 5)
{
  $count++;
```

```
}
$count = 1;
while(($r = $q->fetch()) && $count <= 5)
{
   echo $r['lastName'], '<br>';
   $count++;
}
$q->closeCursor();
$q = null;
```

Here, the first loop is used to skip the necessary starting row and the second loop displays the requested subset of rows.

This approach may work well for small tables, but its performance is not good. You should always use database-specific SQL to return the subset of the resulting rows. If you need database independence, you should examine the underlying database software and issue a query specific to the database. The reason for this is that the database can perform certain optimizations on the query, use less memory so that less data will be exchanged between the server and the client.

Unfortunately, PDO does not provide database-independent ways to effectively fetch subsets of the resulting rows as PDO is a connection abstraction, not a database abstraction, tool. If you need to write portable code, you should explore tools such as MDB2.

This approach may seem more complicated than using the PDOStatement::fetchAll() method. Indeed, we could rewrite the previous code as follows:

```
$stmt = $conn->query("SELECT * FROM authors ORDER BY lastName,
                        firstName");
$page = $stmt->fetchAll(PDO::FETCH_ASSOC);
$page = array_slice($page, 5, 5);
foreach($page as $r)
{
   echo $r['lastName'], '<br>';
}
```

Although this code is much shorter, it has a major drawback: It instructs PDO to return all rows from the table and then take a portion of them. With our approach, the unnecessary rows are discarded and the loop instructs the database to stop sending rows as soon as enough rows have been returned. However, the database has to send us the rows preceding the current page in both cases.

Summary

In this chapter, we have seen how to work with unbuffered queries and to get the row count for a result set. We have also looked at an application where database-specific SQL could not be avoided, as this would require a workaround that might be unsuitable. However, this chapter should be helpful for someone who is developing a complex web application that uses databases.

In the next chapter, we will discuss the advanced features of PDO, including persistent connections and other driver-specific options. We will also discuss transactions and examine some more methods of the PDO and PDOStatement classes.

6
Advanced PDO Usage

Now that we have familiarized ourselves with the basic features of PDO and used them to build a data-driven web applications, let's see some advanced functionality. In this chapter, we will look at getting and setting connection attributes (such as column names, case conversion, and the name of the underlying PDO driver) as well as connecting to a database by specifying a connection configuration filename or an option in the `php.ini` file. We will also discuss transactions.

We will modify our library application to display the name of the database driver in the footer of every page. In addition to this simple change, we will extend the application to keep track of how many copies of a single book we have and to keep track of those people who have borrowed a book. We will use transactions for this functionality.

Setting and Getting Connection Attributes

We have briefly covered setting connection attributes in Chapter 3 when we saw how to use exceptions as a means of error reporting. Connection attributes allow us to control certain aspects of the connection as well as to query such things as the driver name and version.

- One way is to specify an array of attribute name/value pairs in the PDO constructor.
- Another way is to call the `PDO::setAttribute()` method, which accepts two parameters:
    - The attribute's name
    - The attribute's value

In PDO, attributes and their values are defined as constants in the PDO class as in the following call in the common.inc.php file:

```
$conn->setAttribute(PDO::ATTR_ERRMODE, PDO::ERRMODE_EXCEPTION);
```

It includes two such constants—PDO::ATTR_ERRMODE and PDO::ERRMODE_EXCEPTION.

To get the value of an attribute, there is the PDO::getAttribute() method. It accepts a single parameter, the attribute name, and returns the value of the attribute. For example, the following code would print Exception:

```
if($conn->getAttribute(PDO::ATTR_ERRMODE) == PDO::ERRMODE_EXCEPTION) {
   echo 'Exception';
}
```

Now, let's see what connection attributes there are in PDO.

- PDO::ATTR_CASE. This attribute controls the case of column names that are returned by the PDOStatement::fetch() method. It is useful if the fetch mode is PDO::FETCH_ASSOC or PDO::FETCH_BOTH (as when the row is returned as an array that contains columns indexed by their name). This attribute can have one of the following three values: PDO::CASE_LOWER, PDO::CASE_NATURAL, and PDO::CASE_UPPER. Depending on this value, the column names will be lowercase, left without changes, or uppercase, respectively as in the following code snippet:

  ```
  $conn->setAttribute(PDO::ATTR_CASE, PDO::CASE_UPPER);
  $stmt = $conn->query("SELECT * FROM authors LIMIT 1");
  $r = $stmt->fetch(PDO::FETCH_ASSOC);
  $stmt->closeCursor();
  var_dump($r);
  ```

  would print:

  ```
  array(4)
  {
    ["ID"]=>
    string(1) "1"
    ["FIRSTNAME"]=>
    string(4) "Marc"
    ["LASTNAME"]=>
    string(7) "Delisle"
    ["BIO"]=>
    string(54) "Marc Delisle is a member of the MySQL Developers
                 Guild"
  }
  ```

  The default behavior is not to change the column name case, that is PDO::CASE_NATURAL.

- PDO::ATTR_ORACLE_NULLS: This attribute, despite its name, works for all databases, not just Oracle. It controls how the NULL values and empty strings are passed in PHP. The possible values are PDO::NULL_NATURAL (for no transformation to happen), PDO::NULL_EMPTY_STRING (for empty strings to be replaced by PHP's null value), and PDO::NULL_TO_STRING (for the SQL NULL value is converted to an empty string in PHP).

You can see how this attribute works in the following code:

```
$conn->setAttribute(PDO::ATTR_ORACLE_NULLS, PDO::NULL_TO_STRING);
$stmt = $conn->query("SELECT * FROM books WHERE coverImage IS
                      NULL LIMIT 1");
$r = $stmt->fetch(PDO::FETCH_ASSOC);
$stmt->closeCursor();
var_dump($r);
```

Would result with:

```
array(9)
{
  ["id"]=>
  string(1) "2"
  ["author"]=>
  string(1) "2"
  ["title"]=>
  string(18) "ImageMagick Tricks"
  ["isbn"]=>
  string(10) "1904811868"
  ["publisher"]=>
  string(20) "Packt Publishing Ltd"
  ["year"]=>
  string(4) "2006"
  ["summary"]=>
  string(81) "Unleash the power of ImageMagick
          with this fast,friendly tutorial and tips guide"
  ["coverMime"]=>
  string(0) ""
  ["coverImage"]=>
  string(0) ""
}
```

As you can see, the highlighted fields are reported as strings, not NULLs (which would be the case if we didn't set the PDO::ATTR_ORACLE_NULLS attribute).

- PDO::ATTR_ERRMODE. This attribute sets the error reporting mode for the connection. It accepts three values:

  ○ PDO::ERRMODE_SILENT: No action is taken, and the error codes are available via PDO::errorCode() and PDO::errorInfo() methods (or their equivalents in the PDOStatement class). This is the default value.

- ○ `PDO::ERRMODE_WARNING`: As before, no action is taken, but an error will be raised with `E_WARNING` level.
- ○ `PDO::ERRMODE_EXCEPTION` will set the error codes (as with `PDO::ERRMODE_SILENT`), and an exception of class `PDOException` will be thrown.

There are also driver-specific attributes, which we will not cover here. Refer to `http://www.php.net/pdo` for more information. However, there is one driver-specific attribute worth our attention: `PDO::ATTR_PERSISTENT`. You can use it to specify that the MySQL driver should use persistent connections, which gives better performance (You can think of this as a counterpart for `mysql_pconnect()` function.) This attribute should be set in the PDO constructor rather than via a `PDO::setAttribute()` call:

```
$conn = new PDO($connStr, $user, $pass,
                array(PDO::ATTR_PERSISTENT => true);
```

The above three attributes are read/write attributes, which means that they can be read and written. There are also read-only attributes, available only via the `PDO::getAttribute()` method. These attributes may return string values (rather than constants defined in the PDO class).

- `PDO::ATTR_DRIVER_NAME`: This returns the name of the underlying database driver:

  ```
  echo $conn->getAttribute(PDO::ATTR_DRIVER_NAME);
  ```

  This will print either MySQL or SQLite depending on the driver you use.

- `PDO::ATTR_CLIENT_VERSION`: This returns the name of the underlying database client library version. For example, for MySQL this may be something like 5.0.37.

- `PDO::ATTR_SERVER_VERSION`: This returns the version of the database server you are connecting to. For MySQL, this can be a string such as `"4.1.8-nt"`.

Let's now get back to our application and modify it to show the database driver in the footer of every page. To achieve this, we will modify the `showFooter()` function in `common.inc.php`:

```
function showFooter()
{
  global $conn;

  if($conn instanceof PDO) {
    $driverName = $conn->getAttribute(PDO::ATTR_DRIVER_NAME);
    echo "<br/><br/>";
```

```
        echo "<small>Connecting using $driverName driver</small>";
    }
    ?>
    </body>
    </html>
    <?php
}
```

In this function, we are importing the $conn variable from the global namespace. If this variable is an object of the PDO class, then we will call the getAttribute() method as discussed above. We have to do this check because in some situations the $conn variable may not be set. For example, if the PDO constructor fails and throws an exception, we will not be able to call any methods on the $conn variable (this will lead to a fatal error—calling member functions on non-objects are fatal errors.)

Since all pages in our application call the showFooter() method function, this change will be visible everywhere:

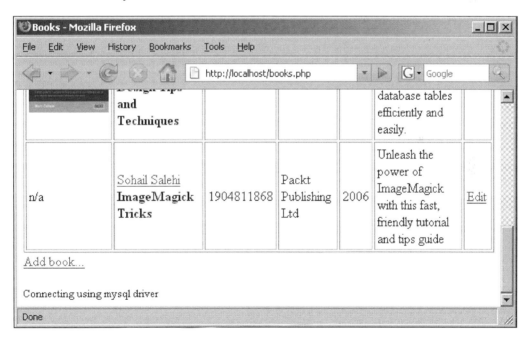

MySQL Buffered Queries

If you are working with a MySQL database only, then you may want to employ MySQL's PDO driver buffered query mode. When the connection is set to the buffered query mode, the whole result set for every SELECT query is pre-fetched into memory before it is returned to the application. This gives us one benefit—we can use the `PDOStatement::rowCount()` method to inspect how many rows the result set contains. In Chapter 2, we discussed this method and showed that it returns 0 for MySQL and SQLite databases. Now, when PDO is instructed to use buffered queries, this method will return meaningful values.

To force PDO into MySQL buffered query mode, you have to specify the `PDO::MYSQL_ATTR_USE_BUFFERED_QUERY` connection attribute. Consider the following example:

```
$conn = new PDO($connStr, $user, $pass);
$conn->setAttribute(PDO::ATTR_ERRMODE, PDO::ERRMODE_EXCEPTION);
```

```
$conn->setAttribute(PDO::MYSQL_ATTR_USE_BUFFERED_QUERY, 1);
$q = $conn->query("SELECT * FROM books");
echo $q->rowCount();
```

This will print the number of rows returned.

Please note that this attribute works for MySQL only and is not portable across databases. You should use it if your application will be working with MySQL only. Also, remember that buffered queries that return large result sets are very expensive with respect to resource and should be avoided. If you are going to use buffered queries, make sure you disable them before issuing such expensive queries. This can be done by turning this attribute off:

```
$conn->setAttribute(PDO::MYSQL_ATTR_USE_BUFFERED_QUERY, 0);
```

You can query whether MySQL buffered queries are currently enabled by calling

```
$conn->getAttribute(PDO::MYSQL_ATTR_USE_BUFFERED_QUERY);
```

I have switched databases for every screenshot (and in the first screenshot the page is scrolled down to the bottom to save space).

Connecting Using the Connection Configuration File and php.ini Setting

When we discussed the connection strings (or the data source names for PDO), we saw that the connection string starts with the driver name followed by a semicolon. PDO also supports configuration files—a file that contains the connection string. For example, we can create a file called `pdo.dsn` in the directory where we can keep the application files and put the connection string there:

```
mysql:host=localhost;dbname=pdo
or
sqlite:/www/hosts/localhost/pdo.db
```

Alternatively, we can create two files, `mysql.dsn` and `sqlite.dsn`, containing the first and the second connection strings respectively.

Then in the PDO constructor, we can specify the configuration file path or URL, not just the connection string:

```
uri:./pdo.dsn
```

PDO will read the file and use the connection string specified there. The advantage of using this method is that you can specify not just a local file, but any URL so that a remote file can be included (provided a suitable stream handler is registered in the system for a protocol such as HTTP or FTP). On the other hand, if the file is not properly protected from web access by all users, then it can potentially leak secure information to a third party, so care should be taken when this method is being used to specify the connection string.

There is also another way of specifying the connection string: in the `php.ini` file. For example, you can define the following directives in the `php.ini` file:

```
pdo.dsn.mysql= mysql:host=localhost;dbname=pdo
pdo.dsn.sqlite=sqlite:/www/hosts/localhost/pdo.db
```

then it is possible to pass 'mysql' or 'sqlite' strings to the PDO constructor instead of the whole connection strings for mysql and sqlite, respectively:

```
$conn = new PDO('mysql', $user, $pass);
$conn = new PDO('sqlite', $user, $pass);
```

As you can see, the connection string in this case should match the corresponding option in the `php.ini` file with the 'pdo.dsn' prefix.

Getting the List of Available Drivers

PDO allows you to programmatically get the list of all installed drivers. The PDO::getAvailableDrivers() method can be called to return an array containing the names of the database drivers that can be used. For example, this code will print something similar to the following:

```
var_dump(PDO::getAvailableDrivers());
array(3)
{
  [0]=>
  string(5) "mysql"
  [1]=>
  string(6) "sqlite"
  [2]=>
  string(7) "sqlite2"
}
```

The names of drivers, contained in this array, are the prefixes for the connection strings. Also, the same name is returned as the value of the `PDO::ATTR_DRIVER_NAME` attribute.

> The `PDO::getAvailableDrivers()` method returns the names of drivers that are registered with the PDO system in the `php.ini` file. You may not be able to use all of these drivers on the local machine—for example, if the MySQL server is not running then the presence of a MySQL item in the returned array does not mean that you can connect to the local MySQL server, and if a certain database server is running on the local machine but its driver is not registered with PDO, then you will not be able to connect to that database server.

Transactions

PDO API also standardises the transaction handling methods. By default, after the successful creation of the PDO connection, it is set to `autocommit` mode. This means that for every database that supports transactions, every query is wrapped in an implicit transaction. For those database that do not support transactions, every query is executed as is.

Typically, the transaction handling strategy is this:

1. Begin the transaction.
2. Wrap the database-related code in a *try...catch* block.
3. The database-related code (within the *try* block) should commit the changes after all the updates have been done.
4. The *catch* block should rollback the transaction.

Of course, only the code that updates the database and the code that can break data integrity should be handled in a transaction. A classic example of a transaction is a money transfer:

1. Begin the transaction.
2. If there is enough money on the payer's account:
   ° Subtract the amount from the payer's account.
   ° Add the amount to the beneficiary's account.
3. Commit the transaction.

If anything bad happens in the middle of a transaction, the database does not get updated and the data integrity is preserved. Also, by wrapping the account balance check into the transaction, we ensure that a concurrent update does not corrupt data integrity.

PDO offers just three methods for transactions handling: `PDO::beginTransaction()` which initiates the transaction, `PDO::commit()` which commits the changes made since the call to `PDO::beginTransaction()`, and `PDO::rollBack()`, which rolls back any changes since the transaction has been initiated.

The `PDO::beginTransaction()` method does not accept any parameters and returns a Boolean value depending on the success of the transaction initiation. If the call to this method fails, then PDO will throw an exception (for example, if you are already in the middle of a transaction, PDO will tell you so). Likewise, the `PDO::rollBack()` method will throw an exception if there is no active transaction, and the same will happen if you call the `PDO::commit()` method before calling `PDO::beginTransaction()`. (Of course, your error handling mode must be set to `PDO::ERRMODE_EXCEPTION` for the exceptions to be thrown.)

You should also be noted that you should not use direct queries to control transactions if you are using PDO for that task. By this, we mean that you should not issue queries such as `BEGIN TRANSATION`, `COMMIT`, or `ROLLBACK` with the `PDO::query()` method. Otherwise, the behaviour of these three methods will be inconsistent. Also, PDO does not currently support savepoints.

Let's now get back to our library application. To see how transactions work in practice, we will modify it by allowing it to track how many copies of a certain book we have, and we will implement a function to keep track of people to whom we have lent books.

This modification will encompass the following changes:

- We will have to alter the books table by adding a new column to keep the number of copies of every book. The `editBook.php` page will need to be modified in order to change this value

- We will create a table to keep track of all borrowers, but to keep the example simple, we will not create a table of borrowers (as we for a real-life library application). We will just associate a borrower's name with the book ID of the book that we have lent them.

- We will create a page that will be used when we lend a book. This page, will ask for the borrower's name and then insert a record into the borrowers table and decrease the number of copies in the books table.

- We will also need a page, which will list all borrowers and another script, which will allow them to return a book. This script will delete a record from the borrowers table and increase the number of copies in the books table.

We will use transactions only when we update two tables at once (as in the last two points in the above list).

Before we do the coding, we will alter the books table:

```
mysql> alter table books add column copies tinyint not null default 1;
Query OK, 3 rows affected (0.50 sec)
Records: 3  Duplicates: 0  Warnings: 0
```

The same command should be executed for SQLite.

Now, let's modify books.php a bit to show how many copies of each book we have and to provide a link. Here are the line of code that will need to be changed (lines 20 to 58):

```
<table width="100%" border="1" cellpadding="3">
<tr style="font-weight: bold">
  <td>Cover</td>
  <td>Author and Title</td>
  <td>ISBN</td>
  <td>Publisher</td>
  <td>Year</td>
  <td>Summary</td>
  <td>Copies</td>
  <td>Lend</td>
  <td>Edit</td>
</tr>
<?php
// Now iterate over every row and display it
while($r = $q->fetch())
{
  ?>
  <tr>
    <td>
      <?php if($r['coverMime']) { ?>
        <img src="showCover.php?book=<?=$r['id']?>">
      <?php } else { ?>
        n/a
      <? } ?>
    </td>
    <td>
      <a href="author.php?id=<?=$r['authorId']?>"><?=htmlspecialchars
                   ("$r[firstName] $r[lastName]")?></a><br/>
      <b><?=htmlspecialchars($r['title'])?></b>
    </td>
```

```
<td><?=htmlspecialchars($r['isbn'])?></td>
<td><?=htmlspecialchars($r['publisher'])?></td>
<td><?=htmlspecialchars($r['year'])?></td>
<td><?=htmlspecialchars($r['summary'])?></td>
<td><?=$r['copies']?></td>
<td>
  <a href="lendBook.php?book=<?=$r['id']?>">Lend</a>
</td>
<td>
  <a href="editBook.php?book=<?=$r['id']?>">Edit</a>
</td>
</tr>
<?php
}
?>
```

Now, for both MySQL and SQLite you should see a page like the following screenshot (where we have scrolled downwards and to the right so that it will fit onto the page):

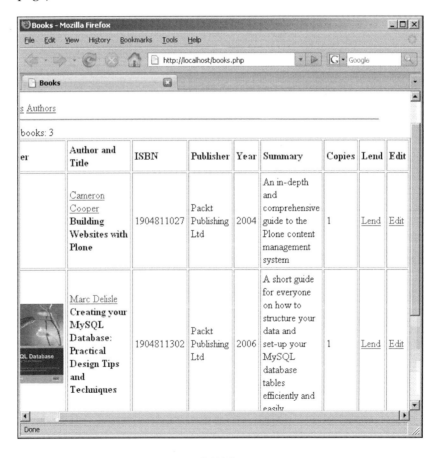

Now, let's create the borrowers table. As we have previously discussed, the table will contain an ID field, the book's ID field, borrower's name, and a timestamp column. We will need an ID (primary key) on this table to prevent possible data corruption; for example, if the same borrower takes the same book twice. If we were tracking borrowers by name and book ID only, then we could have duplicate records in that table and the return of a single book could delete several rows in this table, which would lead to data corruption:

```
mysql> create table borrowers(
    -> id int primary key not null auto_increment,
    -> book int not null,
    -> name varchar(40),
    -> dt int);
Query OK, 0 rows affected (0.13 sec)
```

For SQLite, the syntax will be a bit different:

```
sqlite> create table borrowers(
   ...> id integer primary key,
   ...> book int not null,
   ...> name varchar(40),
   ...> dt int);
```

The page to *lend* the book (`lendBook.php`) is probably the most difficult part. This page will consist of a form where you can enter the borrower's name. Upon successful submission, the script will initiate the transaction, check that there is at least one copy of the book available, insert a record into the borrowers table and decrease the copies column in the books table, commit the transaction, and redirect to the `books.php` page.

```php
<?php
/**
 * This page allows lending a book
 * PDO Library Management example application
 * @author Dennis Popel
 */

// Don't forget the include
include('common.inc.php');

// First see if the request contains the book ID
// Return back to books.php if not
$id = (int)$_REQUEST['book'];
if(!$id) {
  header("Location: books.php");
```

```
      exit;
   }

   // Now see if the form was submitted
   $warnings = array();
   if($_POST['submit']) {
     // Require that the borrower's name is entered
     if(!$_POST['name']) {
       $warnings[] = 'Please enter borrower\'s name';
     }
     else {
       // Form is OK, "lend" the book
       $conn->beginTransaction();
       try
       {
         $stmt = $conn->query("SELECT copies FROM books WHERE id=$id");
         $copies = $stmt->fetchColumn();
         $stmt->closeCursor();
         if($copies > 0) {
           // If we can lend it
           $conn->query("UPDATE books SET copies=copies-1
                       WHEREid=$id");
           $stmt = $conn->prepare("INSERT INTO borrowers(book, name, dt)
                              VALUES(?, ?, ?)");
           $stmt->execute(array($id, $_POST['name'], time()));
         }
         else {
           // Else show warning
           $warnings[] = 'There are no more copies of this book
                       available';
         }
         $conn->commit();
       }
       catch(PDOException $e)
       {
         // Something bad happened
         // Roll back and rethrow the exception
         $conn->rollBack();
         throw $e;
       }
     }
     // Now, if we don't have errors,
     // redirect back to books.php
     if(count($warnings) == 0) {
```

```
      header("Location: books.php");
      exit;
   }
   // otherwise, the warnings will be displayed
}

// Display the header
showHeader('Lend Book');

// If we have any warnings, display them now
if(count($warnings)) {
   echo "<b>Please correct these errors:</b><br>";
   foreach($warnings as $w)
   {
      echo "- ", htmlspecialchars($w), "<br>";
   }
}

// Now display the form
?>
<form action="lendBook.php" method="post">
   <input type="hidden" name="book" value="<?=$id?>">
   <b>Please enter borrower's name:<br></b>
   <input type="text" name="name"value="<?=htmlspecialchars
                                    ($_POST['name'])?>">
   <input type="submit" name="submit" value=" Lend book ">
</form>

<?php
// Display footer
showFooter();
```

Let's run through the code now. We begin by checking that the book's ID has been passed to the script either via the URL or via the form. (We keep the ID in the hidden field of the form.) Then, if there is a form submission (with the submit button pressed), we check that the name field was correctly filled. If the test succeeds, we proceed to the transaction, where we count how many copies are left and check that this number is greater than zero, we decrease the copies column and use a prepared statement to insert a record into the borrowers table. If there is less than one copy, we add a message to the $warnings array so that a warning is displayed on the page.

If there is some failure within the transaction, the catch block will be executed. The transaction will be rolled back and the exception will be thrown again. We do this in order to let our default error handler do its job.

Now, if you save the above code listing in `lendBook.php` and click on one of the **Lend** links on the books listing page, you should arrive at the following page:

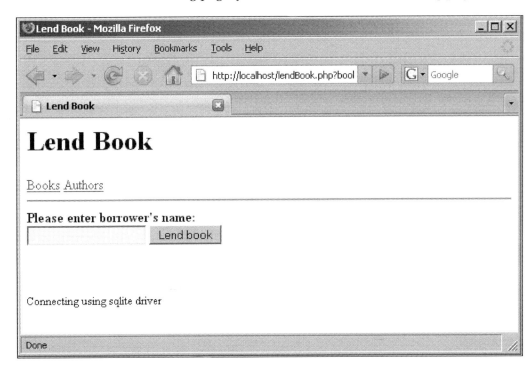

Of course, you should switch between databases to see that the code works with MySQL and SQLite.

To enhance the page, we should also show the title and the author of the book, but we will leave that to you. Also, if you are wondering why we are alerting users that there are no more copies only after the form submission, this is because we can decide on that within the transaction only. If we detect that there are copies available within the transaction, only then we may be assured that no concurrent update will change that. Of course, from the user's perspective, another addition might be a warning displayed along with the book's details. However, a check within the transaction is required too.

Now, if you *lend* a book you will see that the **Copies** column on the books listing page has decreased. Let's now create the page where all the borrowers and the books lent to them will be listed. Let's call it `borrowers.php`. While this page does not process any user input, it contains a query that joins three tables (borrowers, books, and authors):

```php
<?php

/**
 * This page lists all borrowed books
 * PDO Library Management example application
 * @author Dennis Popel
 */

// Don't forget the include
include('common.inc.php');

// Display the header
showHeader('Lended Books');

// Get all lended books count and list
$sql = "SELECT borrowers.*, books.title, authors.firstName,
                authors.lastName
   FROM borrowers, books, authors
   WHERE borrowers.book=books.id AND books.author=authors.id
   ORDER BY borrowers.dt";
$totalBooks = getRowCount($sql);
$q = $conn->query($sql);
$q->setFetchMode(PDO::FETCH_ASSOC);

// now create the table
?>
Total borrowed books: <?=$totalBooks?>
<table width="100%" border="1" cellpadding="3">
<tr style="font-weight: bold">
  <td>Title</td>
  <td>Author</td>
  <td>Borrowed by</td>
  <td>Borrowed on</td>
  <td>Return</td>
</tr>

<?php
// Now iterate over every row and display it
while($r = $q->fetch())
{
  ?>
  <tr>
```

```
      <td><?=htmlspecialchars($r['title'])?></td>
      <td><?=htmlspecialchars("$r[firstName] $r[lastName]")?></td>
      <td><?=htmlspecialchars($r['name'])?></td>
      <td><?=date('d M Y', $r['dt'])?></td>
      <td>
        <a href="returnBook.php?borrower=<?=$r['id']?>">Return</a>
      </td>
    </tr>
    <?php
  }
  ?>
  </table>

  <?php
  // Display footer
  showFooter();
```

The code is easy to follow; it follows the same logic as books.php or authors.php.
However, since this page isn't linked from anywhere, we should add a link to it in
the site header (the showHeader() function in common.inc.php):

```
  function showHeader($title)
  {
    ?>
    <html>
    <head><title><?=htmlspecialchars($title)?></title></head>
    <body>
    <h1><?=htmlspecialchars($title)?></h1>
    <a href="books.php">Books</a>
    <a href="authors.php">Authors</a>
    <a href="borrowers.php">Borrowers</a>
    <hr>
    <?php
  }
```

Now, if you navigate to `borrowers.php`, you should see something like this screenshot:

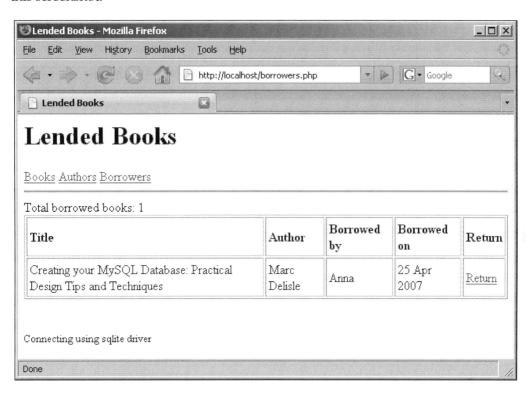

As we can see, this page contains links to the `returnBook.php` page, which does not exist as yet. This script will delete the relevant record from the borrowers table and increment the copies column in the books table. This operation will be wrapped in a transaction, too. Also, `returnBook.php` accepts the borrower's table ID field, (as opposed to `lendBook.php`, which accepted the book's ID). So we should also get the book's ID from the borrowers table:

```php
<?php

/**
 * This page "returns" a book back to the library
 * PDO Library Management example application
 * @author Dennis Popel
 */

// Don't forget the include
include('common.inc.php');

// First see if the request contains the borrowers ID
```

```
// Return back to books.php if not
$id = (int)$_REQUEST['borrower'];
if(!$id) {
  header("Location: books.php");
  exit;
}

// Now start the transaction
$conn->beginTransaction();
try
{
  $q = $conn->query("SELECT book FROM borrowers WHERE id=$id");
  $book = (int)$q->fetchColumn();
  $q->closeCursor();
  $conn->query("DELETE FROM borrowers WHERE id=$id");
  $conn->query("UPDATE books SET copies=copies+1 WHERE id=$book");
  $conn->commit();
  header("Location: books.php");
}
catch(PDOException $e)
{
  $conn->rollBack();
  throw $e;
}
```

The code should be fairly self-descriptive. In the first place we check that the request contains the borrower's ID and then update both tables. Upon successful completion we get redirected to the books listing page, otherwise, the error handler will display a relevant message.

Now, the final touch: the editBook.php page, which can be used to edit how many copies of the book we have. We will leave this to you, but here are some considerations. The suggested way of keeping track of books that have been lent is not very good for a real life library application. Instead of keeping the number of copies available, we should keep the total number of copies in the library in one column and the number of copies that have been lent in another column. This should be done, because editing the number of books available may lead to data corruption. Returning a book will increment the copies column in the books table. If someone else is editing the number of copies available at the same time, they may not know that a borrower is returning a book and hence may enter an incorrect number.

On the other hand, if there were two separate columns, then updating the total number of copies would be completely independent from the updates caused by the books being lent and returned. In this scenario, however, the script that lends a book should check that the number of copies that have been lent is less than the total number of copies. The transaction should continue only if this condition is satisfied.

Summary

In this chapter, we have taken a look at some of the extended functionality offered by PDO, especially transactions. Our application example was modified to provide additional functionality that relies on transactions. We also looked at the organization of the transaction-aware code.

However, as you might have noticed, we were mixing code that updates databases, processes user input, and renders pages in one file. While we tried to keep the input processing and presentation in different parts of one file (first data processing, then page rendering), we could not separate data processing.

In the next chapter, we will see how to separate the data model and the application logic so that the data can be accessed and manipulated from elsewhere, not just from our application. We will develop a data model class that will encapsulate our library application data handling methods. This class can then be used from other applications.

7

An Advanced Example

By now, you should be able to develop web applications with PDO. However, our example application is manageable when it has been kept rather small with limited functionality. Soon you will realize that mixing all the data access, user input, and display logic in one file can become a hassle to manage.

To write a more manageable code and to allow more than one developer to work on a project, the data access user input processing, and page rendering should be separated. You have probably heard of the **Model-View-Controller** programming paradigm (MVC), which is widely used for big web applications. The idea is to keep the data access and modification modules, which is the **Model**, separate from data presentation, which is the **View**. The view can be very complex, so a template engine is usually used. Finally, the **controller** is a PHP script that receives user input, accesses the model, and prepares the view.

In addition to making the code base more manageable, such division allows us to access the functionality of the model from other applications (using maintenance scripts running on either the application's own server or on other servers, which are accessed via RPC or SOAP calls).

As PDO is object-oriented and can return instances of classes from calls to the `PDOStatement::fetch()` method, we will use object-oriented programming to model our data entities (books, authors, and borrowed book records).

Designing the Model

Model is usually comprised of a static class (methods of which are called statically), and several classes that emulate data entities. Calls to the methods of this Model class either return instances of other model classes, or `PDOStatement` instances that return instances of model classes in calls to the `fetch()` method.

For our application, the classes will be Model, Book, Author, and Borrower. These classes reflect the tables in our example database and allow us to perform simple operations on the underlying data. (The main idea is to isolate SQL from the controller scripts into relevant model classes.) For example, the Book class may have a method to return an Author class instance that would represent the author for that book. On the other hand, the Author class might have a method to return a list of Book class instances representing each book written by that author.

In this chapter, we will develop our own static Model class along with the Book, Author, and Borrower classes. Before we begin, we should clearly define what methods (functionality) every class will have. Let's define the functionality of the model.

Model class should contain static methods that will act as *entry points* to the data stored in the database. Such methods should do the following:

- Get all the books.
- Get all the authors.
- Get all the book borrowers.
- Get the number of books.
- Get the number of authors.
- Get the number of book borrowers.
- Get a book by ID.
- Get an author by ID.
- Get a borrower by ID.

On the other hand, the Model class will not contain methods that are performed on a book or on an author. To lend a book, we will use a method defined in the Book class, and to return a book, we will use a method in the Borrower class.

Let's now plan the methods for the Book class:

- Get the author.
- Get a list of the book's borrowers.
- Lend a book.

The Author class is even simpler for our example application:

- Get all the books.
- Get the number of books by this author.

Finally, there is the `Borrower` class that represents a record in the borrowers table:

- Get the book.
- Return the book.

The properties of every data entity will be accessible as instance variables of the relevant class. Also, the methods in these classes will contain PDO calls that we have already written in `books.php` and other files. We will move these methods to the relevant classes, and these files will just act as controllers that process user input. Form validation will still be the task of the controller scripts. However, we are not going to separate the display logic from the business logic, since our application is very simple, and there is no need to use any template engine or even to move the page rendering code into a separate **include** file.

In addition to that, we will not be using the global `$conn` variable any more. The `Model` class will have a private static variable of the same name and a method to retrieve the connection object. This method will follow the singleton pattern and create the object on demand if it's not yet created or simply return it if it's already intitialized (For more information on the singleton pattern and an example implementation in PHP5 you can visit `http://en.wikipedia.org/wiki/Singleton_pattern`.

We will keep all the classes in a separate file, `classes.inc.php`, which will then be included from `common.inc.php`.

Let's begin with the central `Model` class:

```
/**
 * This is the central Model class. Use its static methods
 * To retrieve a book, author, borrower by ID
 * Or all the books, authors and borrowers
 */
class Model
{
  /**
   * This is the connection object returned by
   * Model::getConn()
   * @var PDO
   */
  private static $conn = null;

  /**
   * This method returns the connection object.
   * If it has not been yet created, this method
   * instantiates it based on the $connStr, $user and $pass
```

```
     * global variables defined in common.inc.php
     * @return PDO the connection object
     */
    static function getConn()
    {
      if(!self::$conn) {
        global $connStr, $user, $pass;
        try
        {
          self::$conn = new PDO($connStr, $user, $pass);
          self::$conn->setAttribute(PDO::ATTR_ERRMODE,
                                    PDO::ERRMODE_EXCEPTION);
        }
        catch(PDOException $e)
        {
          showHeader('Error');
          showError("Sorry, an error has occurred. Please
            try your request later\n" . $e->getMessage());
        }
      }
      return self::$conn;
    }

    /**
     * This method returns the list of all books
     * @return PDOStatement
     */
    static function getBooks()
    {
      $sql = "SELECT * FROM books ORDER BY title";
      $q = self::getConn()->query($sql);
      $q->setFetchMode(PDO::FETCH_CLASS, 'Book', array());
      return $q;
    }

    /**
     * This method returns the number of books in the database
     * @return int
     */
    static function getBookCount()
    {
      $sql = "SELECT COUNT(*) FROM books";
      $q = self::getConn()->query($sql);
      $rv = $q->fetchColumn();
```

```
      $q->closeCursor();
      return $rv;
  }

  /**
   *This method returns a book with given ID
   * @param int $id
   * @return Book
   */
  static function getBook($id)
  {
      $id = (int)$id;
      $sql = "SELECT * FROM books WHERE id=$id";
      $q = self::getConn()->query($sql);
      $rv = $q->fetchObject('Book');
      $q->closeCursor();
      return $rv;
  }

  /**
   * This method returns the list of all authors
   * @return PDOStatement
   */
  static function getAuthors()
  {
      $sql = "SELECT * FROM authors ORDER BY lastName, firstName";
      $q = self::getConn()->query($sql);
      $q->setFetchMode(PDO::FETCH_CLASS, 'Author', array());
      return $q;
  }

  /**
   * This method returns the number of authors in the database
   * @return int
   */
  static function getAuthorCount()
  {
      $sql = "SELECT COUNT(*) FROM authors";
      $q = self::getConn()->query($sql);
      $rv = $q->fetchColumn();
      $q->closeCursor();
      return $rv;
  }

  /**
   *This method returns an author with given ID
```

```php
 * @param int $id
 * @return Author
 */
static function getAuthor($id)
{
  $id = (int)$id;
  $sql = "SELECT * FROM authors WHERE id=$id";
  $q = Model::getConn()->query($sql);
  $rv = $q->fetchObject('Author');
  $q->closeCursor();
  return $rv;
}

/**
 * This method returns the list of all borrowers
 * @return PDOStatement
 */
static function getBorrowers()
{
  $sql = "SELECT * FROM borrowers ORDER BY dt";
  $q = self::getConn()->query($sql);
  $q->setFetchMode(PDO::FETCH_CLASS, 'Borrower', array());
  return $q;
}

/**
 * This method returns the number of borrowers in the database
 * @return int
 */
static function getBorrowerCount()
{
  $sql = "SELECT COUNT(*) FROM borrowers";
  $q = self::getConn()->query($sql);
  $rv = $q->fetchColumn();
  $q->closeCursor();
  return $rv;
}

/**
 *This method returns a borrower with given ID
 * @param int $id
 * @return BorrowedBook
 */
static function getBorrower($id)
{
  $id = (int)$id;
```

```
        $sql = "SELECT * FROM borrowers WHERE id=$id";
        $q = Model::getConn()->query($sql);
        $rv = $q->fetchObject('Borrower');
        $q->closeCursor();
        return $rv;
    }
}
```

As you can see, this class defines the getConn() method that is used to retrieve the PDO connection object, as well as nine more methods — three methods for every data entity (book, author, and borrower). The methods to get all the data entities (getBooks(), getAuthors(), and getBorrowers()) return a PDOStatement pre-configured to fetch instances of relevant classes. The methods to return the number of every data entity, fetch an integer, while the method to return a single data entity, fetch an instance of the data entity model class. Note how we close cursors in these methods — this functionality has been transferred from the controller files.

Let's now look at the three model classes.

```
/**
 * This class represents a single book
 */
class Book
{
    /**
     * Return the author object for this book
     * @return Author
     */
    function getAuthor()
    {
        return Model::getAuthor($this->author);
    }

    /**
     * This method is used to lend this book to the person
     * specified by $name. It returns the Borrower class
     * instance in case of success, or null in case when we cannot
     * lend this book due to insufficient copies left
     * @param string $name
     * @return Borrower
     */
    function lend($name)
    {
        $conn = Model::getConn();
```

```
        $conn->beginTransaction();
        try
        {
          $stmt = $conn->query("SELECT copies FROM books
                               WHERE id=$this->id");
          $copies = $stmt->fetchColumn();
          $stmt->closeCursor();
          if($copies > 0) {
            // If we can lend it
            $conn->query("UPDATE books SET copies=copies-1
              WHERE id=$this->id");
            $stmt = $conn->prepare("INSERT INTO borrowers(book, name, dt)
                                   VALUES(?, ?, ?)");
            $stmt->execute(array($this->id, $name, time()));
            // Success, get the newly created
            // borrower ID
            $bid = $conn->lastInsertId();
            $rv = Model::getBorrower($bid);
          }
          else {
            $rv = null;
          }
          $conn->commit();
        }
        catch(PDOException $e)
        {
          // Something bad happened
          // Roll back and rethrow the exception
          $conn->rollBack();
          throw $e;
        }
        return $rv;
      }
    }
```

Here we have just two methods. One is used to get the book's author. (Note how we reuse the `Model::getAuthor()` method here.) Another method provides the *lend book* functionality. Note how we reread the copies column from the database rather than rely on the `$this->copies` variable. As we have seen in the previous chapter, this is done to ensure data integrity. The `$this->copies` variable gets assigned long before the transaction begins, and by the time that the `Book::lend()` method is called, the actual count of copies in the database might have changed.

That's why we reread that value inside the transaction again. Also, this method returns null if the operation fails or an instance of Borrower class if the operation is successful. If an error occurs, an exception gets thrown that is handled by the exception handler defined in common.inc.php (just as it did previously).

Another model class is Author. It's very simple:

```
/**
 * This class represents a single author
 */
class Author
{
  /**
   * This method returns the list of books
   * written by this author
   * @return PDOStatement
   */
  function getBooks()
  {
    $sql = "SELECT * FROM books WHERE author=$this->id
                      ORDER BY title";
    $q = Model::getConn()->query($sql);
    $q->setFetchMode(PDO::FETCH_CLASS, 'Book', array());
    return $q;
  }

  /**
   * This method returns the number of books
   * written by this author
   * @return int
   */
  function getBookCount()
  {
    $sql = "SELECT COUNT(*) FROM books WHERE author=$this->id";
    $q = Model::getConn()->query($sql);
    $rv = $q->fetchColumn();
    $q->closeCursor();
    return $rv;
  }
}
```

These two methods just return the list of books written by this author and the number of books in this list.

Finally, the `Borrower` class represents a record in the borrower's table:

```php
/**
 * This class represents a single borrower
 * (i.e., a record in the borrowers table)
 */
class Borrower
{
  /**
   * Return the book associated with this borrower
   * @return Book
   */
  function getBook()
  {
    return Model::getBook($this->book);
  }

  /**
   * This method "returns" a book.
   * After this method call, this object
   * is unusable as it does not represent
   * a data entity any more
   */
  function returnBook()
  {
    $conn = Model::getConn();
    $conn->beginTransaction();
    try
    {
      $book = $this->getBook();
      $conn->query("DELETE FROM borrowers WHERE id=$this->id");
      $conn->query("UPDATE books SET copies=copies+1
                    WHERE id=$book->id");
      $conn->commit();
    }
    catch(PDOException $e)
    {
      $conn->rollBack();
      throw $e;
    }
  }
}
```

Essentially, the body of the `returnBook()` method is transferred from the `returnBook.php` file (just as the `Book::lend()` method was transferred with a slight modification from the `lendBook.php` file).

Modifying the Frontend to Use the Model

Now that we have removed the data access logic from the files that generate frontend pages, let's see how we should modify them. Let's start with the `books.php` file:

```php
<?php

/**
 * This page lists all the books we have
 * PDO Library Management example application
 * @author Dennis Popel
 */

// Don't forget the include
include('common.inc.php');

// Display the header
showHeader('Books');

// Get the books list
   $books = Model::getBooks();

// now create the table
?>
Total books: <?=Model::getBookCount()?>
<table width="100%" border="1" cellpadding="3">
<tr style="font-weight: bold">
  <td>Cover</td>
  <td>Author and Title</td>
  <td>ISBN</td>
  <td>Publisher</td>
  <td>Year</td>
  <td>Summary</td>
  <td>Copies</td>
  <td>Lend</td>
  <td>Edit</td>
</tr>

<?php
// Now iterate over every row and display it
while($b = $books->fetch())
{
  $a = $b->getAuthor();
```

```
    ?>
    <tr>
      <td>
        <?php if($b->coverMime) { ?>
          <img src="showCover.php?book=<?=$b->id?>">
        <?php } else { ?>
          n/a
        <? } ?>
      </td>
      <td>
        <a href="author.php?id=<?=$a->id?>"><?=htmlspecialchars("$a
                              >firstName $a->lastName")?></a><br/>
        <b><?=htmlspecialchars($b->title)?></b>
      </td>
      <td><?=htmlspecialchars($b->isbn)?></td>
      <td><?=htmlspecialchars($b->publisher)?></td>
      <td><?=htmlspecialchars($b->year)?></td>
      <td><?=htmlspecialchars($b->summary)?></td>
      <td><?=$b->copies?></td>
      <td>
        <a href="lendBook.php?book=<?=$b->id?>">Lend</a>
      </td>
      <td>
        <a href="editBook.php?book=<?=$b->id?>">Edit</a>
      </td>
    </tr>
    <?php
}
?>
</table>

<a href="editBook.php">Add book...</a>
<?php
// Display footer
showFooter();
```

As you can see, we have removed the SQL commands and the calls to the PDO class instance methods, and replaced them with corresponding calls to the methods of the Model class. (Note the highlighted lines.)

Another important change is that the instances of the Book class returned in the while loop (starting on line 30) don't have the variables for the author's first or last names. To get these variables, we call the Book::getAuthor() method for every book that we display. Then, later in the loop, we reference either the $b variable to access the book's properties or the $a variable to access the author's details. Note how we access these details as the object variables rather than array elements here.

This happened because the Model::getBooks() method does not employ table joins any more, so the instances of the Book class won't contain author details. Instead, the Book class defines a method to get the Author object for that book. This means that, for every book that we display, we will execute an extra SQL query to get the author's details.

On the first sight this may seem too expensive, performance-wise. But on the other hand, in real life application, we would show just one page (say, 20 books) from a table of several thousand records. In this case, a SELECT statement without JOIN on the books table selecting the rows to be displayed in the current page and followed by some simple queries for every row to be displayed may be more performance-effective.

However, if this approach is inappropriate, then the Model class can be extended with another method, for example, Model::getBooksWithAuthors(), that would return instances of the Book class where the lastName and firstName variables would be present. This method might look like the following:

```
/**
 * This method returns the list of all books with
 * author's first and last names
 * @return PDOStatement
 */
static function getBooksWithAuthors()
{
  $sql = "SELECT books.*, authors.lastName, authors.firstName
        FROM books, authors
        WHERE books.author=authors.id
        ORDER BY title";
  $q = self::getConn()->query($sql);
  $q->setFetchMode(PDO::FETCH_CLASS, 'Book', array());
  return $q;
}
```

Developing the model part may constrain us in terms of flexibility, but this is the price to pay for code manageability. However, this can be overcome with additional methods in the model classes or, if this is really necessary, with direct communication with PDO. The above method is possible because PDO does not care what variables were defined in the class; it just dynamically creates variables for every column returned by the query.

This is a very powerful feature when used responsibly. If not used with care, you may end up with hard-to-track logical errors. For example, if in the above method you selected the ID column from the authors table, then its value would overwrite the ID column value selected from the books table. Other methods in the Book class rely on the value in the id field being correct and may lead to severe data corruption if this value is incorrect.

Another file that we should now modify is authors.php:

```php
<?php
/**
 * This page lists all the authors we have
 * PDO Library Management example application
 * @author Dennis Popel
 */

// Don't forget the include
include('common.inc.php');

// Display the header
showHeader('Authors');

// Get number of authors and issue the query
$authors = Model::getAuthors();

// now create the table
?>
Total authors: <?=Model::getAuthorCount()?>
<table width="100%" border="1" cellpadding="3">
<tr style="font-weight: bold">
  <td>First Name</td>
  <td>Last Name</td>
  <td>Bio</td>
  <td>Edit</td>
</tr>

<?php
// Now iterate over every row and display it
while($a = $authors->fetch())
{
  ?>
  <tr>
    <td><?=htmlspecialchars($a->firstName)?></td>
    <td><?=htmlspecialchars($a->lastName)?></td>
    <td><?=htmlspecialchars($a->bio)?></td>
    <td>
```

```
    <a href="editAuthor.php?author=<?=$a->id?>">Edit</a>
  </td>
 </tr>
 <?php
}
?>
</table>
<a href="editAuthor.php">Add Author...</a>
<?php
// Display footer
showFooter();
```

Here, we just replaced the direct communication with PDO with the call to the `Model` class as well as rewrote the loop to use object variables rather than array elements.

The changes made to the application also allow us to remove SQL-related code bits from `author.php`:

```php
<?php
/**
 * This page shows an author's profile
 * PDO Library Management example application
 * @author Dennis Popel
 */

// Don't forget the include
include('common.inc.php');

// Get the author
$id = (int)$_REQUEST['id'];
$author = Model::getAuthor($id);

// Now see if the author is valid - if it's not,
// we have an invalid ID
if(!$author) {
  showHeader('Error');
  echo "Invalid Author ID supplied";
  showFooter();
  exit;
}

// Display the header - we have no error
showHeader("Author: $author->firstName $author->lastName");

// Now get the number and fetch all his books
$books = $author->getBooks();
```

```php
$totalBooks = $author->getBookCount();

// now display everything
?>
<h2>Author</h2>
<table width="60%" border="1" cellpadding="3">
<tr>
  <td><b>First Name</b></td>
  <td><?=htmlspecialchars($author->firstName)?></td>
</tr>
<tr>
  <td><b>Last Name</b></td>
  <td><?=htmlspecialchars($author->lastName)?></td>
</tr>
<tr>
  <td><b>Bio</b></td>
  <td><?=htmlspecialchars($author->bio)?></td>
</tr>
<tr>
  <td><b>Total books</td>
  <td><?=$totalBooks?></td>
</tr>
</table>
<a href="editAuthor.php?author=<?=$author->id?>">Edit author...</a>

<h2>Books</h2>
<table width="100%" border="1" cellpadding="3">
<tr style="font-weight: bold">
  <td>Title</td>
  <td>ISBN</td>
  <td>Publisher</td>
  <td>Year</td>
  <td>Summary</td>
</tr>
<?php
// Now iterate over every book and display it
while($b = $books->fetch())
{
  ?>
  <tr>
    <td><?=htmlspecialchars($b->title)?></td>
    <td><?=htmlspecialchars($b->isbn)?></td>
    <td><?=htmlspecialchars($b->publisher)?></td>
    <td><?=htmlspecialchars($b->year)?></td>
```

```
    <td><?=htmlspecialchars($b->summary)?></td>
  </tr>
  <?php
}
?>
</table>

<?php
// Display footer
showFooter();
```

The changes here are rather cosmetic, as it just removes the direct communication with PDO and changes to the *object* syntax from the *array* syntax on highlighted lines.

Finally, the last page that shows a list from `borrowers.php`:

```php
<?php

/**
 * This page lists all borrowed books
 * PDO Library Management example application
 * @author Dennis Popel
 */

// Don't forget the include
include('common.inc.php');

// Display the header
showHeader('Lended Books');

// Get all lended books list
$brs = Model::getBorrowers();
$totalBooks = Model::getBorrowerCount();

// now create the table
?>
Total borrowed books: <?=$totalBooks?>
<table width="100%" border="1" cellpadding="3">
<tr style="font-weight: bold">
  <td>Title</td>
  <td>Author</td>
  <td>Borrowed by</td>
  <td>Borrowed on</td>
  <td>Return</td>
</tr>

<?php
// Now iterate over every row and display it
while($br = $brs->fetch())
```

```php
{
  $b = $br->getBook();
  $a = $b->getAuthor();
  ?>
  <tr>
    <td><?=htmlspecialchars($b->title)?></td>
    <td><?=htmlspecialchars("$a->firstName $a->lastName")?></td>
    <td><?=htmlspecialchars($br->name)?></td>
    <td><?=date('d M Y', $br->dt)?></td>
    <td>
      <a href="returnBook.php?borrower=<?=$br->id?>">Return</a>
    </td>
  </tr>
  <?php
}
?>
</table>

<?php
// Display footer
showFooter();
```

In this file, we have the same problem as we had with `books.php` page—the `Model` class returns instances of the `Borrower` class without the book title and the author name, which we want to display on this page. Because of that, we get the `Book` class instance for each `Borrower` class instance on every iteration, and then use that object to get author details.

Finally, we will modify two more pages to make use of our newly created data model. These two are `lendBook.php` and `returnBook.php`. They probably contained the longest bit of code that interfaced with PDO. From `lendBook.php` we remove all the code wrapped within the transaction:

```php
<?php
/**
 * This page allows you to lend a book
 * PDO Library Management example application
 * @author Dennis Popel
 */

// Don't forget the include
include('common.inc.php');

// First see if the request contains the book ID
// Return to books.php if the ID invalid
```

```php
$id = (int)$_REQUEST['book'];
$book = Model::getBook($id);
if(!$book) {
  header("Location: books.php");
  exit;
}

// Now see if the form was submitted
$warnings = array();
if($_POST['submit']) {
  // Require that the borrower's name is entered
  if(!$_POST['name']) {
    $warnings[] = 'Please enter borrower\'s name';
  }
  else {
    // Form is OK, "lend" the book
    if(!$book->lend($_POST['name'])) {
      // Failure, show error message
      $warnings[] = 'There are no more copies of
                    this book available';
    }
  }

  // Now, if we don't have errors,
  // redirect back to books.php
  if(count($warnings) == 0) {
    header("Location: books.php");
    exit;
  }
  // Otherwise, the warnings will be displayed
}

// Display the header
showHeader('Lend Book');

// If we have any warnings, display them now
if(count($warnings)) {
  echo "<b>Please correct these errors:</b><br>";
  foreach($warnings as $w)
  {
    echo "- ", htmlspecialchars($w), "<br>";
  }
}

// Now display the form
?>
<form action="lendBook.php" method="post">
```

```
    <input type="hidden" name="book" value="<?=$id?>">
    <b>Please enter borrower's name:<br></b>
    <input type="text" name="name" value="<?=htmlspecialchars($_
                                        POST['name'])?>">
    <input type="submit" name="submit" value=" Lend book ">
</form>

<?php
// Display footer
showFooter();
```

Note how we changed the part that *lends* the book—the Bool::lend() method returns null in case of failure, so we will display a message that there are no more books left to lend. If the operation is successful, then Book::lend() method returns the Borrower class instance (which evaluates to true in the if statement) and the page redirects to books.php.

Similarly, we remove the PDO-related code from returnBook.php and replace it with the corresponding call to the Borrower::returnBook() method:

```
<?php

/**
 * This page "returns" a book back to the library
 * PDO Library Management example application
 * @author Dennis Popel
 */

// Don't forget the include
include('common.inc.php');

// First see if the request contains the borrowers ID
// Return to books.php if not
$id = (int)$_REQUEST['borrower'];
$borrower = Model::getBorrower($id);
if(!$borrower) {
  header("Location: books.php");
  exit;
}

// Return the book and redirect to books.php
// If anything happens, the exception will be
// handled automatically
$borrower->returnBook();
header("Location: books.php");
```

Advantages of Separating the Model

So far, almost all of the files that generate front-end pages don't contain data access logic and are easier to manage. On the other hand, the model classes can be used from outside our application, and additional pages can be quickly created to represent the information in the database in other formats such as XML.

For example, consider the following page (which we will call `books.xml.php`):

```php
<?php
/**
 * This page lists all the books we have as an XML data structure
 * PDO Library Management example application
 * @author Dennis Popel
 */

// Don't forget the include
include('common.inc.php');
// Set the content type to be XML
header('Content-Type: application/xml');
// Get the books list
$books = Model::getBooksWithAuthors();

// Echo XML declaration and open root element
echo '<?xml version="1.0"?>', "\n";
echo "<books>\n";

// Now iterate over every book and display it
while($b = $books->fetch())
{
  ?>
  <book id="<?=$b->id?>">
    <isbn><?=$b->isbn?></isbn>
    <title><?=htmlspecialchars($b->title)?></title>
    <publisher><?=htmlspecialchars($b->publisher)?></publisher>
    <summary><?=htmlspecialchars($b->summary)?></summary>
    <author>
      <id><?=$b->author?></id>
      <lastName><?=$b->lastName?></lastName>
      <firstName><?=$b->firstName?></firstName>
    </author>
  </book>
  <?
}
echo '</books>';
```

This file allows us to export the list of books in XML format for another application. As you can see, the changes to the original `books.php` file are only in the display logic. If you now navigate to the page, you should see the following:

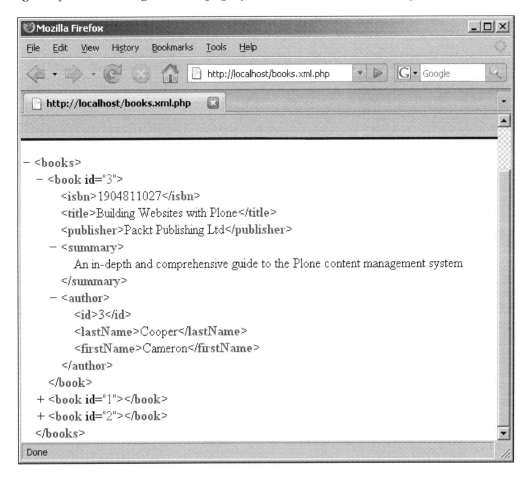

With a slight modification, we were able to create new representation of our data (The second and third books have been collapsed to fit everything on the screenshot).

Another advantage of defining `model` classes is that these classes become the central point for data access and manipulation. For example, if you change the SQL for representing data from several tables (using joins) or find a way to optimize a query, you just have to update the relevant model class, and the scripts (controllers) that were using that query don't have to get updated. This is a major manageability advantage.

You may extend abstract model classes to imitate extended functionality for real subclasses in a common data model. For example, in a content management system you can create an abstract base class called Item, which will have common properties for all the subclasses (item types) such as author, keywords, and creation date. Then the model can perform some operations for all possible subclasses without further coding so that the existing code is extensively reused.

There are tools called **object-relational mappers** (ORMs) that make use of the ideas described in this chapter. ORMs are used to create powerful object-oriented applications where you have virtually no SQL code in you model. (In fact, these tools after some configuring play the role of the model in your application.) You can read more about ORMs at http://en.wikipedia.org/wiki/Object-relational_ mapping. Propel (http://propel.phpdb.org/) is a popular ORM tool for PHP5.

Further Thoughts

The model developed in this chapter, needs some improvements in at least two areas, if you want to use it in a real-life application. We didn't create methods in the model that would provide the functionality of the editBook.php and editAuthor.php files. However, you should now be ready to add this functionality by yourself. We will provide you with some tips:

- Create the Book::update() and Author::update() methods. These methods should accept parameters that reflect the properties of each object (for the Author class, this should be first name, last name, and biography).

- These methods should use prepared statements to update the corresponding records in the database (based on the $this->id value).

- The Model class should be extended with two more methods, Model:: createBook() and Model::createAuthor(). These methods should accept the same list of parameters as Book::update() and Author::update(). Both should insert a row based on the passed parameters, into the relevant table. This can be done with the following code:

```
$conn = self::getConn();
$conn->beginTransaction();
try
{
  $conn->query("INSERT INTO authors(bio) VALUES('')");
  $aid = $conn->lastInsertId();
  $author = self::getAuthor($aid);
  $author->update($firstName, $lastName, $bio);
  $conn->commit();
}
```

```
catch(Exception $e)
{
    $conn->rollBack();
}
```

The idea here is to concentrate entity updating in a single place, namely `Author::update()`. We employ a transaction here to ensure that, if anything happens, the empty row is not stored in the database.

- The form processing code should detect whether it's editing an existing entity or creating a new one and call `Model::createAuthor()` or `Author::update()` on an already existing instance appropriately.

Another problem is that, the methods of the model classes do not validate accepted parameters. They should provide validation of every parameter passed to the database if you are going to expose your data model to third-party applications. If accessed via web browser, our data model is protected by the form validation code. However, direct access to the model classes is not as secure.

It is advisable to throw an exception from the model methods that accept user-supplied parameters in case the validation fails. Also, web form validation and method parameter validation should use common code. (For example, you might develop a `Validation` class that could be used to validate values regardless of where they come from.) This code should be used from within the form validation code and model methods. By doing this, so you will assure code reuse and a single place for the validation rules.

Finishing Up

PHP Data Objects is a great and easy-to-use technology. However, it's still in its infancy and many improvements and other changes are yet to come. Be sure to keep yourself updated with the latest news from PHP developers and from the large community of PHP fans and users.

Effective use of PDO and PHP in general, is possible only with a sound understanding of security threats and how to protect against them. Using PDO's prepared statements diminishes the risk of SQL injection attacks, but you, the developer, are still responsible for securing your application. Make sure that you keep track of the latest developments in the security field.

Happy PHP-ing!

A
Introduction to OOP in PHP5

Throughout this book, we were mainly using procedural code to build the example application. However, the PDO API is fully object-oriented, and in the last chapter we imitated real-life entities in the database by using classes. This appendix is for those programmers who are not familiar with PHP5's object-oriented extensions. We will introduce you to the basics of OOP, as many developers coming from earlier versions of PHP have no experience of this type of programming. However, this is only a short introduction; if you want to master OOP, you should refer to some of the books devoted to this topic.

What is Object-Oriented Programming?

Object-oriented programming (OOP) is a relatively new concept, although its roots date back to 1960s. In OOP, the software works with objects that model real-life entities (such as books and authors in the Chapter 7). Whereas procedural programming involves a series of instructions, an application in OOP involves a set of objects that interact with each other.

The Syntax for Declaring Objects

An object can be viewed as a container for several variables, called properties, and for functions that act on these variables. These functions are called methods. Every object belongs to a class. In PHP, every object can belong to only one class (although some other OOP languages allow multiple inheritance), but there can be many objects, or instances, belonging to a single class. A class is a syntactic construct that allows you to describe what properties and methods the objects belonging to this class will have.

There is an analogy with species and living organisms—for example, a Dog (a species, or a class) is a generalization of all living dogs. A generalized dog has such properties as weight and age, and a method such as bark, and a real-life dog, say Lessie, which belongs to the dog species, could be described as an instance of the Dog class.

Let's see how we would model this in PHP5:

```
class Dog
{
   public $weight;
   public $age;

   function bark()
   {
      print "woof!";
   }
}

$lessie = new Dog();
$lessie->weight = 15;
$lessie->age = 3;
$lessie->bark();
```

In this small snippet of code, we defined a class called Dog. In PHP5, a class definition starts with the reserved word class followed by the class's name (A class's name can contain the same characters as a function's name.) All the class's properties and methods, collectively called **members**, are defined inside the {...} block.

As you can see, we are using the keyword, public, when we declare properties and methods. In PHP4 we would have used the var keyword instead, but this keyword is deprecated in PHP5. Besides the public keyword, we could have used the protected keyword or the private keyword, but more on this later.

As you can see in the second part of the code, we create the object with the new keyword:

```
$lessie = new Dog();
```

This line creates a new object belonging to the Dog class and assigns it to the $lessie variable. This is a very important step, since this is the only way to create objects. After the PHP processes it, the $lessie variable becomes initialized and we can access the properties and methods declared in the Dog class so that we act on the object called Lessie. We would now like to have two dogs in our application, and the second one will be called K9. To achieve that, we would have to write something like this:

```
$k9 = new Dog();
$k9->age = 5;
$k9->weight = 18;
```

Now, we can access both the `$k9` and `$lessie` variables, if we would like to interface with each of our dogs.

In other words, before we can communicate with an instance, it first has to be created with the `new` keyword.

After the variable has been initialized, we can access its properties and methods. As you can see in the code, this is achieved with the `->` construct, which is used with both properties and methods. Note that when accessing a class's properties, we don't have to write the dollar sign after the -> (but we have to use it when declaring the properties inside the class definition).

The methods are declared with the `function` keyword followed by the method's name and a list of parameters. In fact, a class's methods are declared in a similar way to that for an ordinary function, but there is one major difference. Inside the declaration of a method, there always exists implicit variable, called `$this`, which allows you to access the object's properties. Let's see how we could create a `getInfo()` method to return some additional information about our dogs:

```php
<?php

class Dog
{
  public $weight;
  public $age;

  function bark()
  {
    print "woof!";
  }

  function getInfo()
  {
    return 'Weight: ' . $this->weight . ' kg, age: ' . $this->age .
                                                ' years';
  }
}

$lessie = new Dog();
$lessie->weight = 15;
$lessie->age = 3;
```

```
$k9 = new Dog();
$k9->age = 5;
$k9->weight = 18;
echo 'Lessie: ', $lessie->getInfo(), "\n";
echo 'K9: ', $k9->getInfo(), "\n";
```

This code would display the following output:

```
Lessie: Weight: 15 kg, age: 3 years
K9: Weight: 18 kg, age: 5 years
```

Constructors

Every class also has a special function (which may be implicit or explicitly declared) called a **constructor**. The constructor is always called when PHP encounters the new keyword, and its purpose is to perform some initialization tasks. Let's extend the Dog class so that it has a $name property. We will also change the code so as to initialize the name, weight, and age properties inside the constructor rather than in the main application:

```php
<?php
class Dog
{
  public $weight;
  public $age;
  public $name;

  function __construct($name, $age, $weight)
  {
    $this->name = $name;
    $this->weight = $weight;
    $this->age = $age;
  }

  function bark()
  {
    print "woof!";
  }

  function getInfo()
  {
    return
      'Name: ' . $this->name .
      ', weight: ' . $this->weight .
      ' kg, age: ' . $this->age .
      ' years';
```

```
    }
}
$lessie = new Dog('Lessie', 3, 15);
$k9 = new Dog('K9', 5, 18);

echo $lessie->getInfo(), "\n";

echo $k9->getInfo(), "\n";
```

This application would display the following:

```
Name: Lessie, weight: 15 kg, age: 3 years
Name: K9, weight: 18 kg, age: 5 years
```

Here's a brief summary of what we did. We first declared the $name property and then the constructor for our Dog class. The constructors are declared as function with the special name of __construct (the word constructor prepended with two underscores('_'). Our constructor accepts three parameters—name, age, and weight, whose values are assigned to the object's properties. The order in which we assign values to the properties does not matter. Note that we always have to use the $this variable to denote the properties of the object. By doing this, we can differentiate the local variables $name, $age, and $weight (passed as parameters) from the object's own properties, which have the same names, inside the constructor.

We also changed the getInfo() method so that it returns the name of the dog as well. We can now instantiate objects by passing the name, the age, and the weight to the constructor. Since these properties get assigned in the constructor, we don't have to do this in the main part of the code.

It should be also noted that you can assign default values to properties in the class definition. This will ensure that every object of that class will have the default values automatically assigned. For example, we can do the following:

```
class Dog
{
  public $weight;
  public $age;
  public $name;
  public $hasCollar = true;

  function __construct($name, $age, $weight)
  {
    $this->name = $name;
    $this->weight = $weight;
    $this->age = $age;
```

```
    }
    function bark()
    {
       print "woof!";
    }
    function getInfo()
    {
       return
         'Name: ' . $this->name .
         ', weight: ' . $this->weight .
         ' kg, age: ' . $this->age .
         ' years, has collar: ' . ($this->hasCollar ? 'yes' : 'no');
    }
 }
```

If you run the application with this Dog class definition, then you will see the following output:

```
Name: Lessie, weight: 15 kg, age: 3 years, has collar: yes
Name: K9, weight: 18 kg, age: 5 years, has collar: yes
```

As you can now see, the default property value for hasCollar has propagated to every newly created instance (of course, it can be later changed for each object).

Destructors

There is an opposite concept to constructors, called destructors. As its name suggests, destructors are used to perform cleanup tasks (classic examples of such tasks are deleting temporary files, closing database connections, etc). In PHP5, destructor on an object is called, when there are no more references to that object (for example, by setting the variable that holds the reference to the object to **null** or when the application terminates), then the destructor will be called.

Destructor is a method: __destruct(). If you add that method to the class, then it will be called when the object is freed. Let's add the destructor to the **Dog** class:

```
class Dog {
   public $weight;
   public $age;
   public $name;
   public $hasCollar = true;

   function __construct($name, $age, $weight) {
```

```
    $this->name = $name;
    $this->weight = $weight;
    $this->age = $age;
  }

  function bark() {
    print "woof!";
  }

  function getInfo() {
    return
      'Name: ' . $this->name .
      ', weight: ' . $this->weight .
      ' kg, age: ' . $this->age .
      ' years, has collar: ' . ($this->hasCollar ? 'yes' : 'no');
  }

  function __destruct() {
    print "Freeing $this->name\n";
  }
}
```

Now, if you run the code again, it will give the following output:

```
Name: Lessie, weight: 15 kg, age: 3 years, has collar: yes
Name: K9, weight: 18 kg, age: 5 years, has collar: yes
Freeing K9
Freeing Lessie
```

Note that the order in which PHP5 calls the destructors is not defined. Also, in a destructor, the code may not access other objects unless they are referenced by the object being freed. In other words, the destructor should only cleanup those resources that were created by that object.

The Advantages of OOP

The power of OOP lies in its three main characteristics: inheritance, encapsulation, and polymorphism.

Inheritance

Inheritance in OOP allows you to create new classes that inherit an existing class's behaviour (methods) and attributes (properties). Let's consider the following example. Assume that we have a class called `Fruit`. It is a generalized type of class for different fruits, and its common attributes are color and weight. In OOP, we can subclass `Fruit` to create new classes `Apple` and `Banana`. Both these classes (being subclasses of Fruit) will have the same properties: `weight` and `color`. (Note we are speaking about properties as such, not about their values). An apple can have a green color, while a `Banana` can have a yellow color. But any code that interacts with `Apple` or `Banana` class instances does not need to know what kind of fruit it is communicating with.

Let's put this example into code:

```
class Fruit
{
  public $color;
  public $weight;
}

class Apple extends Fruit
{
  function __construct()
  {
    $this->color = 'green';
    $this->weight = 200;
  }
}

class Banana extends Fruit
{
  function __construct()
  {
    $this->color = 'yellow';
    $this->weight = 250;
  }
}

$a[] = new Apple();
$a[] = new Banana();
foreach($a as $f)
{
  echo $f->color, "\t", $f->weight, "\n";
}
```

As you can see, in this small application we have one `Apple` object and one `Banana` object. We iterate over them in a loop, but access their properties regardless of their type, since both classes use the same property names. But these properties carry different values for each fruit.

Inheritance also allows to extend or completely override the behavior of the parent classes. Let's assume that our `Fruit` class has one more characteristic—price per kg. It also has a new method—`getPrice()` that just multiplies the weight (which we have in grams) by the price:

```
class Fruit
{
  public $color;
  public $weight;
  public $price;

  function getPrice()
  {
    return $this->weight / 1000 * $this->price;
  }
}
```

Now we can use this method in the subclasses:

```
class Apple extends Fruit
{
  function __construct()
  {
    $this->color = 'green';
    $this->weight = 200;
    $this->price = 2;
  }
}

class Banana extends Fruit
{
  function __construct()
  {
    $this->color = 'yellow';
    $this->weight = 250;
    $this->price = 3;
  }
}

$a[] = new Apple();
$a[] = new Banana();
foreach($a as $f)
```

```php
{
  echo $f->getPrice(), "\n";
}
```

Next, we will assume that the Banana class has another method for calculating price so that a discount is applied:

```php
class Banana extends Fruit
{
  function __construct()
  {
    $this->color = 'yellow';
    $this->weight = 250;
    $this->price = 3;
  }

  function getPrice()
  {
    return $this->weight / 1000 * $this->price * 0.9;
  }
}
```

As you can see, we changed the method in the Banana class so that the code calling the Banana class's implementation of the getPrice() method will get discounted price, while the Apple class's getPrice() method returns full price.

On the other hand, we could reuse the Fruit class's implementation of the getPrice() method in the Banana class (so that we don't have to duplicate the code contained in the base class):

```php
function getPrice()
{
  return parent::getPrice() * 0.9;
}
```

Encapsulation

Encapsulation (sometimes called information hiding) is a more theoretical concept. It involves defining methods in a class in such a way that we hide the implementation details from the client code. We have already seen this when we redefined the price calculation in the Banana class. From the application's point of view, nothing changed: we still call the getPrice() method, but we don't know how this calculation is performed.

In other words, classes are accessible through their methods, which have the same names so that, even if the code behind these names changes, the names themselves do not change. This ensures that existing code does not need to be changed to work with new versions of methods.

We can do more to hide implementation details from client code, PHP5, like other object-oriented languages, supports **visibility modifiers** for methods and properties. For example, we could add a private property, which will be hidden from the rest of the application, to the Banana class:

```
class Banana extends Fruit
{
  private $mySecretProperty;
  function __construct()
  {
    $this->color = 'yellow';
    $this->weight = 250;
    $this->price = 3;
  }

  function getPrice()
  {
    return parent::getPrice() * 0.9;
  }
}
```

The $mySecretProperty property is only accessible (or visible) in the Banana class; an attempt to access it from outside the Banana class's methods would trigger a run-time error. (In a compiled language, this would lead to a compilation error.)

In PHP5, there exist two more modifiers: **public** (which we have already used), and **protected**. Public method or property is accessible from all the application, while protected is accessible inside the class and its subclasses only.

Polymorphism

Polymorphism is a feature of OOP that allows us to write code that will work with objects belonging to different classes provided that these classes have the same base class. We have already seen polymorphism in action in the above example when we were accessing properties and methods of different objects using their names but returning different values and taking different actions.

The subclasses implement all the properties and methods belonging to the base class, and all future subclasses of the base class are guaranteed to implement these properties and methods so that the existing code can work even with subclasses which do not yet exist.

PHP5 supports interfaces. An interface is a construct that describes certain behaviour in different classes and class hierarchies. For example, let's consider a `Tradeable` interface that has a single method, `isImported()`:

```
interface Tradeable
{
  public isImported();
}
```

Now, we can declare in the definition of the `Fruit` class that it implements the Tradeable interface:

```
class Fruit implements Tradeable
{
  public $color;
  public $weight;
  public $price;

  function getPrice()
  {
    return $this->weight / 1000 * $this->price;
  }

  function isImported()
  {
    return false;
  }
}
```

We have made `Fruit` objects and all objects belonging to its subclasses (`Apple` and `Banans`) non-imported by default. Now we can make bananas imported while leaving apples domestic:

```
class Banana extends Fruit
{
  function __construct()
  {
    $this->color = 'yellow';
    $this->weight = 250;
    $this->price = 3;
  }

  function getPrice()
  {
    return parent::getPrice() * 0.9;
  }

  function isImported()
  {
    return true;
  }
}
```

Next we will create an imaginary `Car` class that implements the `Tradeable` interface:

```
class Car implements Tradeable
{
  public $year;
  public $make;
  public $model;

  function isImported()
  {
    return true;
  }
}
```

Note that `Car` does not extend `Fruit`, but it still has the `isImported()` method. Now we can call this method from the application:

```
$a[] = new Apple();
$a[] = new Banana();
$a[] = new Car();
foreach($a as $item)
{
  echo $item->isImported();
}
```

This small example shows how objects from different class hierarchies can be treated in the same way by giving them a common interface. By doing this, objects that normally have quite different meanings can be manipulated in the same way, and this makes them polymorphic.

Static Properties, Methods, and Class Constants

In all the examples in this appendix, we are using instances (objects) of classes, which modeled real-life entities. However, in PHP5 it is possible to use **static** properties and methods. Static properties are variables that are common to all the instances of the given class so that, if a static property is changed, it will get changed for all objects belonging to the class.

A static property is declared just like a regular one, but with a special **static** keyword:

```
class DataModel
{
  public static $conn = null;
}
```

The static properties can be accessed without even creating an instance of the class:

```
if(!DataModel::$conn) {
    echo 'Connection not established!';
}
```

The syntax for accessing a static property is as follows: the class name, then double semicolon, and then the property's name. Note that with static properties (unlike with regular properties), the dollar sign, $, sign must be present.

Static methods, just like static properties, can be accessed without instantiating an object. They are declared and accessed in the following way:

```
class DataModel
{
    public static $conn = null;

    static function getConn()
    {
        if(!DataModel::$conn) {
            DataModel::$conn = new PDO('sqlite:./my.db', 'user', 'pass');
        }
        return DataModel::$conn;
    }
}

$conn = DataModel::getConn();
```

The declaration of a static method has the static keyword followed by a regular method declaration. The method is accessed by the class name followed by a double semicolon and then the method name.

The static properties and methods can be accessed inside the class declaration using the shortcut keyword self:

```
class DataModel
{
    public static $conn = null;
    static function getConn()
    {
        if(!self::$conn) {
            self::$conn = new PDO('sqlite:./my.db', 'user', 'pass');
        }
        return self::$conn;
    }
}

$conn = DataModel::getConn();
```

There is also a major difference with the definition of static methods. You cannot use the $this variable (as there is no object to which the $this variable can refer).

Another 'static' feature of classes is class constants. A class constant acts like a static property, but its value cannot be changed. Class constants always must have their values assigned in the class declaration section, and they don't have the dollar sign before them (so they are named just like regular PHP constants). Class constants are mostly used for keeping the global namespace cleaner (which is also one of the uses for static methods):

```
class DataModel
{
  public static $conn = null;
  const ORDER_AZ = 1;
  const ORDER_ZA = 2;

  static function getConn()
  {
    if(!self::$conn) {
      self::$conn = new PDO('sqlite:./my.db', 'user', 'pass');
    }
    return self::$conn;
  }

  static function getItems($sortMode)
  {
    if($sortMode == self::ORDER_AZ) {
      $sql = // SQL for ascending
    }
    else {
      $sql = // SQL for descending
    }
  }
}

$items = DataModel::getItems(DataModel::ORDER_ZA);
```

An attempt to assign a value to a class constant in the code will lead to a parse error.

Exceptions

As we have seen, exceptions are a very important addition to PHP5. Exceptions are special kind of object that, when instantiated and thrown, break the normal execution flow and jump to a so called catch block.

Exceptions are used to report error conditions. Traditionally, functions return error codes if they fail. The application has to check every function call before proceeding to the next function call. Remember the piece of code that you use to connect to a MySQL database:

```
$dbh = mysql_connect($host, $user, $pass);
if(!$dbh) {
    die('Could not connect to the DB!');
}

if(!mysql_select_db('mydb')) {
    die('Could not select the DB');
}

$q = mysql_query('SELECT * FROM test');
if(!$q) {
    die('Could not execute query');
}

while($r = mysql_fetch_row($q))
{
    ...
}
```

If the `mysql_xxx` functions could throw exceptions, this code could be simplified to this:

```
try
{
    mysql_connect($host, $user, $pass);
    mysql_select_db('mydb');
    $q = mysql_query('SELECT * FROM test');

    while($r = mysql_fetch_row($q))
    {
        ...
    }
}
catch(Exception $e)
{
    die(e->getMessage());
}
```

Of course, this code would not work, as these functions are not designed to throw exceptions. You will have to use PDO, and in Chapter 3 we saw how to work with PDO exceptions.

Exceptions allow you to postpone error checking and maintain cleaner code. A function (or method) that causes an exception to be thrown is terminated, and the code in the block specified by the `catch` keyword is executed. Any code that might throw an exception is wrapped into the `try` block:

```
try
{
   // do something exceptional
}
catch(Exception $e)
{
   // display warnings etc
   // $e->getMessage() contains error message
}
```

The real power of exceptions is the ability to escalate them up the call stack. This means that, if you design a function or class method that can throw an exception, that function or method does not have to catch that exception. In fact, many application libraries are designed in such a way so that they don't process exceptions themselves, but instead let them pass to the calling code.

For example, many of the methods of the `PDO` and `PDOStatement` classes that we have encountered in this book can throw exceptions, and it is your responsibility to catch them and act appropriately.

Take a closer look at the `catch` block in the above code snippet. It is followed by the word `Exception` (which is the name of the base class for all exceptions in PHP) and the variable identifier `$e`. We can use the `$e` variable inside the `catch` block to inspect the error message and other debug information. The `Exception` class defines the following methods:

- `getMessage()` returns the error message.
- `getCode()` returns the error code.
- `getFile()` returns the name of the file where the exception occurred.
- `getLine()` returns the number of the line where the exception occurred.
- `getTrace()` and `getTraceAsString()` return the backtrace (call stack), useful for debugging.

Of course, the error messages and error codes vary depending on where the exception occurred, so that they depend on which application library (such as PDO) you use.

We specified the `Exception` class name after the `catch` keyword, because this class, like other classes, can be extended to create subclasses. For example, all exceptions that are thrown from PDO methods are instances of the `PDOException` class.

The exception handling mechanism allows us to create different handling routines for different classes of exception. For example, we can do the following:

```
try
{
    $conn = new PDO('sqlite:./mydb', '', '');
    $q = $conn->query('SELECT * FROM test');

    while($r = $q->fetch())
    {
        ...
    }
}
catch(PDOException $pdoe)
{
    die('Database error: ' . $pdoe->getMessage());
}
catch(Exception $e)
{
    die('Unexpected error: ' . $e->getMessage());
}
```

This code defines two error handling routines for all PDO errors: one class for a database error and another class for all other errors, which we identify as unexpected errors. Of course, in real life applications, the error handling strategies would be more complicated, but this example shows how exceptions can be classified.

Summary

In this appendix, we saw that PHP5 has some new OOP extensions that are comparable with those of modern programming languages. They allow us to write very big applications while maintaining code reuse and cleanliness. Object-oriented programming is a natural solution for big projects such as content management systems or database libraries involving PDO. Libraries for PHP5 are now being written with object-oriented programming in mind.

However, this appendix just gives a short introduction to the main concepts behind OOP so that you can follow the code examples in this book. If you want to fully master object-oriented programming, you should refer to books that will introduce you to and guide you through this challenging topic.

Index

PHP Web 2.0 Mashup Projects

ISBN: 978-1-847190-88-8   Paperback: 250 pages

Create practical mashups in PHP grabbing and mixing data from Google Maps, Flickr, Amazon, YouTube, MSN Search, Yahoo!, Last.fm, and 411Sync.com

1. Expand your website and applications using mashups

2. Gain a thorough understanding of mashup fundamentals

3. Clear, detailed walk-through of the key PHP mashup building technologies

4. Five fully implemented example mashups with full code

Building Websites with XOOPS

ISBN: 1-904811-28-0   Paperback: 180 pages

Get your XOOPS website up fast using this easy-to-follow guide

1. Simple and practical guide to XOOPS

2. Manage blocks, modules, users, and themes

3. Case study reinforces effective learning

Please check **www.PacktPub.com** for information on our titles

Made in the USA
Lexington, KY
29 September 2012